The Art
of being Belgian

Brussels, Belgium and Beyond

Richard Hill

A division of Europublic

Visit the Europublic site at the following address:
www.europublic.com

Published by Europublications, Division of Europublic sca/cva,
  P O Box 504,
  B-1180 Brussels.
  Tel: + 32 2 343 77 26, Fax: + 32 2 343 93 30.

  E-mail: mail@europublic.com

Cover design: Wendy Robinson.
Illustration, page 26: Cathy Walker.
Typography and layout: Hilaire Pletinckx.

Printed in Belgium. Enschede, Brussels.
D/2005/6421/1   ISBN 90744400150

By the same author

WeEuropeans

EuroManagers & Martians

Great Britain Little England

Have You Heard This One?

Us & Them

The NewComers: Austria, Finland and Sweden

Sharks & Custard

Contents

Brussels, Belgium and Beyond

1. Moving over...

"Heavy Fog Over Channel, Continent Cut Off."

Attributed to The Times newspaper

I got into the culture business by what could be called a process of osmosis. Being by nationality British, and culturally English, I started off at a disadvantage. There are some countries which, by reason of their demography or history, tend to be more hermetic culturally than others. Britain is one of them (although the Old Country has opened up a lot since those days), France another and Germany, in a different kind of way, a third.

But I was lucky with my family. Even before WWII my father worked in an international environment and was always coming back from France, Germany, Italy or Belgium with toys for me, and stories of life in these countries for anyone who would listen. So I had, at an impressionable age, the opportunity to 'look over the fence' and realise that there was another world outside the British Isles.

The result was that, at school and university, I concentrated on foreign literature and languages: there were no courses in international relations or cross-cultural management in those days. In addition to economic science, of which I gained only the faintest and rapidly outdated appreciation, I studied French, German and Spanish. When I finally landed a job – foreign languages were of little perceived value to the British in those days – I worked in the export business, first in marketing, then in an international communications consultancy.

Even in those early days I realised – as did my fellow-Brits, most of whom didn't speak a word of any language other than English – that something strange was going on beyond the straits of Dover. An organisational research study produced the, for us, rather startling claim from a German company that "our firm has been functionally organised for the last 95 years" – a fine sentiment, but not what was to have been expected in a world of change. In response to a question on my company's job application form about the position he was applying for, a young Swiss applicant answered "as close to a window as possible."

My first direct and most memorable cross-cultural experience was when I acted as an interpreter in negotiations between a French company and a British one that happened to be a client of the advertising agency I was working for at the time. I was brought in by the Brits, of course, but I don't recollect that they cheated by not declaring my allegiance. Anyway halfway through the negotiations, which were tough, both sides agreed to an adjournment (an indispensable feature of such affairs). I just happened to find myself in the same corner as the French delegates and I was taken aback when they started discussing their strategy openly in front of me.

I had to conclude that either they were so self-absorbed in a French kind of way that they were not even aware of my presence, or that they quite reasonably assumed that I, as a Brit, had no chance of understanding their language. As it happens I spoke reasonably fluent French by that time, so I was able to advise the British delegation on a solution that was ultimately to the benefit of both parties. As I have confirmed many times since, the lasting deals are the win-win ones.

Maybe because I got used to the idea of expecting the unexpected, I have never been particularly prone to culture shock, although I did experience one case of it, as I will explain later. On the contrary, I have been disappointed when new circumstances have failed to challenge me. Like a lot of people I have met in the meantime, I thrive on the unexpected – what I call 'the narcotic of the exotic'. I lived for a couple of years in southern Austria, a year in western Switzerland and part of the year in Spain, and they were all just wonderfully different from what I had been used to at home.

Everything happens ten years later...

Most of us have our personal relocation stories to tell. Mine came in the late-1960s, when I was uprooted from a cosy assignment in the UK to start a continental venture on a shoestring. I owed the opportunity very much to the fact that, out of some 500 people in the British operation, I was the only one who spoke any European language other than English (a lot of Brits don't even realise that English is a European language!).

Anxious to avoid getting trapped in another hermetic culture like the English one – which automatically ruled out France and Germany – I narrowed my choice of location to the Netherlands, Switzerland and Belgium. There was no chance of getting a working permit in Switzerland and, as for the Netherlands, I didn't fancy the food (what food, you might ask?). So I picked Belgium, a decision that produced the usual ribald response from my Dutch friends: "You made a wise choice... If there's going to be a nuclear war, it's best to be in Belgium. Everything happens there ten years later than anywhere else!"

This, of course, was before the Berlin Wall came down. What my Dutch friends didn't realise was that the same joke, minus the nuclear bit, had already been used by Dr Johnson and Heinrich Heine... about the Dutch! Moreover they were not entirely right about Belgium: the Belgians were still knocking down fine buildings faster than anyone else.

My continental European start-up, although it was the product of an Anglo-American joint venture, didn't qualify for corporate multinational treatment. Thus it was that I arrived one stormy October evening on the Ostend ferry with a truckload of second-hand office furniture, my employer having decided that this was the best he could do for me. He had also very considerately engaged the services of an import agency to help me get my truckload through customs. This turned out to be a man on a bicycle who, deterred by the foul weather on the Belgian coast, arrived so late that the customs office was already closed for the night. I drove on to Brussels, disgusted.

The following day I learned that, contrary to my boss's and the man-on-the-bicycle's expectations, the full rate of import duty had been charged on my cast-off furniture. A few days later I also learned that the pound sterling, my principal source of income at the time, had been devalued by 15 percent.

By now, my relocation looked more like a dislocation – complicated by the fact that, at that time, my mother-country was not yet a member of the European Community. When I applied in the French-speaking commune of Ixelles for a *carte professionnelle* to allow me to practise my trade, I was told this could only be done subsequent to my getting a *permis de séjour* but, when I applied at another office in downtown Brussels for my *permis de séjour*, I was told that I first had to get a carte professionnelle!

Such experiences put me in a kafkaesque frame of mind where I began to wonder if I really existed. They also convinced me that, while social contact with Belgians is fine if you can achieve it, the real problem (as in many other countries) is the administrative interface. Officials are known to take cover behind phrases like "that's impossible!" or, more frequently, "we've never done it like that!" – in Flemish or French, or both, or even English (they're great linguists). Such phrases would resound from the 'administrative interface' which, in the case of one commune, took the form of individual counters proudly identified (in French, Flemish and supposedly English) as 'Guichet/Loket/*Wicket* N° 1', etc. Maybe the Belgians did invent cricket after all (see Chapter 5).

Soon, however, I was learning that there was more than one way of getting things done in my newly adopted country. This was brought home to me by the comment of the man issuing me with an identity card: "Can you please give me an estimate of your means? It doesn't have to be true - but don't say I said so." That gave me an early clue to the accommodating nature of the Belgian character. I also discovered very soon, as a relatively young and budding employer, that Belgians are intelligent, sensible and assiduous workers.

Another eye-opener came a bit later when I was helping negotiate the closure of a plant in the Walloon town of Boussu. A government minister sent a letter urging my client to rethink his decision. Below the signature were the words "P.S. please be aware of the fact that I am also the mayor of Boussu." Things don't happen like that these days, thanks to legislation governing the accumulation of mandates.

Surreal confrontations with government administrations – federal, regional and local –are a common experience, particularly for expatriates. A Canadian I know went to his commune for a foreigner's identity card and was told that he had to apply for a formal appointment (or be 'convoked', in administrative lingo). He asked how to apply, and the official said the quickest way would be by phone. So the Canadian went out to the lobby where there was a public phone and called back to the office he had just left. He got an appointment right away – much to the surprise and disgruntlement of the official when he presented himself a few seconds later...

Surrealism is inevitably a feature of a country where it is difficult to take anything for granted. Imagine going into a maternity ward anywhere else and being greeted with the injunction "no admittance to children under 14 years!" *("L'accès des services de maternité est strictement interdit aux enfants de moins de 14 ans).*

Shortly after I arrived in Belgium I also came to the conclusion that anyone with a French-sounding name was likely to be a Flemish-speaker and vice versa. This is a habit I have not entirely thrown off even today.

No doubt it reflects the turbulent history of a country where, until the 18th century, the official language of Flanders was French and the official language of Brabant, where Brussels is located, was Flemish. To add to the general confusion, the phrase *Pays-Bas* ('Low Countries'), which is now used by French speakers to denote the Netherlands, was until the French Revolution the official title of what is today Belgium...

Food and fondness for the surreal

I soon saw what my Dutch friends meant by saying that things happened here ten years late. Within weeks, I was made emphatically aware that the Belgians had, in a number of respects, a time lag of even more than a decade. This was most noticeable in matters of food. They were still getting over the fact that, nearly 25 years earlier, they had been obliged to eat what they could get, and not what they wanted (the Belgian national war museum has an exhibit depicting a wartime household, the most significant feature of which, next to the clandestine BBC broadcast coming over the family radio, is a half-empty larder...).

In the 1960s the Belgians were still suffering – and indeed still are – from a collective *Nachholbedarf*, a delightful German word that puts in a nutshell the concept of 'the need to catch up'. This explained the enormous helpings to be had in the plethora of restaurants in all the main cities, and also the fact that some Belgians were still living off the illegal hoards of food they had stockpiled during the occupation a quarter of a century earlier (so much for the war museum's half-empty larder!).

All this – and the realisation that the Belgians are a very literal-minded people with a great fondness for the surreal – was brought home to me on my first visit to a Brussels cinema. The film was one of André Delvaux' masterpieces and the spectators were almost exclusively solid Brussels bourgeois (it was difficult to find anyone else those days unless you headed for a working-class suburb). They were passive until more than halfway through the film – either through apathy or because they couldn't follow the Bergman-like plot – when, all of a sudden, the camera panned to a table laden with good fare. Pandemonium broke out.

Literal-mindedness and fondness for the surreal: you might think these strange bedfellows would be uncomfortable sharing the same psyche, yet they cohabit readily enough in the average Belgian head. The literal-mindedness also reflects the mercantile spirit that can even get the better of the Belgians' essentially good nature. No less than Leon Tolstoy talked about "Belgianisation – the abandonment of national responsibility in favour of totally commercial values."

I had an early example of this when a contemporary of mine, also a British expatriate, went on a house hunt in the Waterloo area. Told the rent the Belgian proprietor expected of him, he exclaimed: "but we're not Americans." Immediately the proprietor's demands dropped by more than 30 per cent...

I was offered another example when taking my first tram ride in Brussels. This was in the days when the driver was still called a *wattman*, and children ceded their seats to pensioners. A small boy tried to do just that and his mother slapped him and said "Don't get up, I've paid for your seat!" (*"Ne bouge pas, j'ai payé ta place!).*

But back to that fondness for the surreal. It insinuates its way, often unintentionally, into everyday life. I still marvel over the pretensions of business names and their tangled translation into English with the emphasis, for some strange reason, on the power of the possessive apostrophe. Names like Plush's House (*La Maison de la Peluche)*, Baroqu's Pub, Bingo's Palace, Gobelins Art (n.b. no apostrophe), Sign's Rescue (maintenance of illuminated displays), Belgian's Partners, and Shoe's Victim (what?). I even came across a product pack with the proud inscription 'Belgium's Made'. It was a welcome return to reality to discover that Belgium's biggest demolition contractor was actually called Froidcoeur ('cold heart').

Belgian surrealism also goes along with Belgian beers which, I quickly discovered, are delicious. A lot of the finer beers bear the names of saints or monks (many of them being abbey-brewed, this is to be expected) but there are also some surprises at the other end of the spectrum: Mort Subite ('Sudden Death'), Delirium Tremens, Pecheresse ('Sinful Woman'), Paranoia and the like. Having tasted some of these beers, their names may not be as surreal as I thought. If you want to know more about Belgian beer, go to: *http://www.dma.be/p/bier/2_1_uk.htm#L.*

Company names at the time also showed signs of strain, ranging from the poetic (e.g. La Thermogène) to the ludicrous and, to an English speaker's ear, slightly humorous: two of my favourites were the Cobelfret transport organisation, the Sodever waste disposal research laboratory and Coprobat, a building cleaning services company that sounded both dirty and sinister. Fantasy, perhaps unintended, is still at work today: who would have thought of calling an express courier service 'Boomerang' (return to sender?) or a door-to-door catering service 'Brussel's Cold Food' (yuck, and note the apostrophe again)?

There is also still a sizeable stable of companies with names ending in 'bel', as a way of tipping you off as to their origins. Glaverbel, Spacebel, Habitabel and – hold on to your seat – Sodibel come to mind. But I am still searching the records for company names like 'Lapoubel' (think French), Pachebel (a German composer as it happens) and 'Tinckerbel' (got it?).

I also needed a bit of time to get used to the way French-speaking Belgians, with the help of the French, have adopted or distorted the English language: words like *standing* meaning status, *footing* meaning jogging,, boogies (on trains), *bobby traps* (sounds intriguing) and *aquaplanning* (swimming pool design?). Other masterpieces included talkie-walkie (maybe more logical than the English, but now in any case outdated by the cellphone) and *cock-a-little-doo* (definitely not an English bird).

Other early impressions of Belgium were the dubious state of Brussels streets, the sight and sound of grown men kissing one another noisily (generally a clue to the fact that they were French speakers) and, with the help of the cold-hearted Froidcoeur, the absence at the time of any concern for the environment. This was evident in the vast quantities of worthless publicity and free sheets hand-dropped through my letterbox. I also marvelled at the strange inability of Belgian high-street entrepreneurs to resist the temptation to locate their businesses in the same place as their most successful competitors – and thereby bankrupt the lot.

An intriguing aspect of Brussels life was the contrast between the beautifully behaved children and the badly behaved dogs. Dog behaviour has certainly improved since then: the amount of canine refuse left about these days is nothing compared with the tonnages deposited in places like Berlin. Also, with the advance of technology, the sight of poorly bred pooches exercised on endlessly extensible leads by Brussels ladies can be very entertaining, especially when a pedestrian comes round a corner and trips over the lead.

I soon managed to overcome my initial reactions to Brussels which *The Economist*, obviously thinking of the area around the European institutions, described as "that often gloomy and rainswept city." The truth is that Brussels boasts some extremely colourful quarters and, while it runs close to the Netherlands for rainfall, cannot produce anything to compare with the life-threatening downpours I had previously experienced in London.

Battlefields and culture shock

Coming from post-austerity Britain, one of the first things I noticed was the size of the cars here – an early clue to the comfort-loving propensity of the Belgians but one which, today, is no longer much in evidence: in those days any good Brussels bourgeois who could afford it would be floating around in an oversized and overpriced American limousine. Flanders, on the other hand, seemed to be obsessed with *Fietsers*: it was only when I nearly ran into one that I realised these were cyclists and not pedestrians (at that time I was still relying on my very elementary powers of linguistic deduction).

After I had been in the country for about a month, having recovered from my experience with the original man-on-a-bicycle, I plucked up the courage to make my first excursion by car outside Brussels. I decided to drive along the *Chaussée de Waterloo* – even today one of the most dangerous roads in the country – to visit the small town of that name.

The next 40 minutes were more action-packed than an X-rated horror movie. I passed the body of a motorcyclist lying under a car, two cars that had collided head-on, and another car on fire in a roadside ditch. If this was intended to be my 'welcome to Belgium', it left a deep impression on me. I also quickly learned that any English impulse to cede the passage to a pedestrian or another motorist was likely to be rewarded with a bump in what the British call the 'boot'.

Maybe that is why now, 35 years later with drivers' licenses and driving tests part of the regulatory landscape, I find the Belgians are no worse (and no better) than motorists from any other corner of continental Europe. In fact they are now as respectful of the rights of pedestrians as the British are: maybe this provides an insight into the essentially conciliatory nature of the Belgian mind. The only things I really object to are the young professional women in black trouser suits who loutishly assert their superiority behind the wheel of black VW Golfs, and the occasional middle-class housewife in the passenger seat of the family limousine who thinks it her duty to defend her partner by being excessively abusive.

There are a couple of infamous and admittedly badly cambered corners in the *Bois de la Cambre/Terkamerenbos* on the outskirts of Brussels that regularly claim victims who drive too fast and lose control. The police and the city's works department seem to do nothing about this, apart from replacing the kerbstones from time to time. Rumour has it that the arrangement provides a valuable source of income for the towing and car repair people.

But back to Waterloo: in addition to being a small town, it was also the site of a great battle (some of my fellow-countrymen are unaware of the fact). For me the Lion Monument has only one thing in its favour – the view from the top. It may be a *morne plaine* but there are some pleasant vistas, especially to the southeast. Battlefields have never been a hobby of mine (unlike some of my compatriots), so it is agreeable to note how unimportant they are to most Belgians. This lack of respect or total disregard for things they consider to be historical irrelevances reflects the attitude of their ancestors at the time these events occurred: namely to get on with life and pretend they didn't happen.

I, on my side, tend to associate Waterloo with the work of a Victorian British foundry master who named his cast iron cisterns after the place. This struck me as being unusually inspired – in a generation that was renowned for its apparent correctness – until, on researching the subject, I found that his 19th century competitors had come up with such gems as 'The Thunderer' and 'The Deluge'. Who said the Victorians didn't have a sense of fun? 'Thos. Crapper's Patent Waterfall', on the other hand, was simply stating the facts since it was indeed the work of a Thomas Crapper (for more details, please refer to his biography, *"Flushed With Pride"*).

Belgium has often been described as 'the cockpit of Europe'. 'BROM' – Blenheim, Ramillies, Oudenaarde, Malplaquet – is a mnemonic that used to be taught at English schools to help memorise the victories of the great Duke of Marlborough in the War of the Spanish Succession. I was reminded of this when I found myself by accident in the pleasant little Flemish town of Oudenaarde: English schoolteachers have, for once, shown due respect for history by identifying the town by its correct Flemish name. Emboldened by this discovery, I searched the map and found Ramillies which when I got there (it's in the middle of the French-speaking Hesbaye) turned out to be an abandoned and rusting railway junction.

Malplaquet I came across quite by chance. When I stumbled across it, it was still the site of a secondary frontier crossing marking the border between Belgium and France. The only thing to distinguish the site was a ramshackle customs post - and a ramshackle French customs official.

Blenheim I just couldn't find at all. It was only years later that I discovered, history not being my strong point at school, that Marlborough had first trounced the French and Bavarians at a village of this name on the banks of the Danube, before moving north to finish the job in what was later to become Belgium.

How *not* to stage a counter-revolution

Not long after arriving in Belgium, I found myself travelling back from a business appointment in Germany in a railway dining car. The place was packed with French-speaking males who looked unreasonably and uncomfortably 'normalised' with their ill-fitting suits and their toothbrush hairstyles. I was intrigued, so I shared a table with one of them and we got into conversation: from his accent he was unmistakably French, as were his colleagues. My curiosity turned to suspicion: something very odd was going on. When we arrived at Brussels' South station, I followed my fellow-travellers at a discreet distance as they exited through a side door into a street at the back of the station where, sure enough, they piled into a convoy of buses and – as I suspected and was able to conclude the next day when I opened my paper – headed for the French frontier. It was the 30th May 1968 and, the day before, de Gaulle had made a moonlight flit to Germany to rally his general command. To avoid the direct confrontation with student demonstrators that could have resulted if these officers had moved straight from Germany into France, they chose to make this detour through Belgium – but with really very little real effort to conceal their identity.

Belgium has its uses.

The importance of eye contact

Enough of battlefields. Today the enemy is culture shock. My experience of it when it eventually hit me - and it gets everyone sooner or later – came from a totally unexpected angle. Something meaningful had changed in my life, but

No book on Belgium would be complete without a reference to the culinary speciality with which the country is most readily associated: the humble but most exemplary Belgian *frite*. Here is what the official federal website has to say on the subject:

Une frite mayonnaise! There can be few Belgians who have never said this phrase. Because frites or French fries occupy a special place in the culinary culture of the country.

If there is such a thing as a symbol of Belgium, then it is the frite. Its origins are, however, relatively obscure. The term "French fries" seems to attribute this culinary invention to our French neighbours. "Wrong!" reply the purists, "frites were invented in Belgium." According to popular belief, this recipe was first used in the Meuse valley, between Dinant and Liège. The poor inhabitants of this region had the custom of accompanying their meals with small fried fish, but when the river was frozen and they were unable to fish, they cut potatoes lengthwise and fried them in oil to accompany their meals.

There is just as much uncertainty about the invention of frites as about the date when they began to be sold commercially. In 1861, a Belgian entrepreneur called Frits is said to have opened a stand selling this product. He is

also said to have given it its own name. So why do our English-speaking friends call them French fries?

The justification given most often dates from World War I. The American and English Allied troops tasted this dish when they met up with Belgian soldiers whose working language was French, which led to the confusion. Thus they returned with the recipe for French fries. In Belgium frites are eaten accompanied by all sorts of sauces at frite stands or frit kots. And to obtain crispy frites, the Belgians have a secret: cooking the frites not once, but twice in oil.

This Belgian speciality has exported itself extremely well. The French adore eating steak frites salade. The Americans recently discovered genuine Belgian frites with the opening in New York of several friteries based on the Belgian model and run by Belgians.

And then Belgian private enterprise, exploiting its natural sense of marketing, kicks in: *"There will be a marketing event for the first time in Belgium to mark the 50th anniversary of Vanreusel's Snacks NV/SA, the deep fried snack specialists, which employs 150 and has a turnover of 24 million. They will present 100 Smarts in the company's livery to their customers, who specialise in French fries; the cars can be used for a period of two years. This media event is not only economically interesting, because this means that Vanreusel has bought 10% of the Smarts sold in Belgium; it is also an attractive idea. The event is being held on May 30 at 14:00 hrs at Kasteel Marktgraaf, Kastanjedreef 59 in Kalmthout. There is live music and a police escort."*

Press release, May 2005

it took me about three months to realise what it was. Every morning and evening I would walk between home and office – not more than five minutes each time – and I would feel I was a ghost. I was totally deprived of the casual eye contact with passers-by that I was used to from my years in London.

This kind of cultural nuance is insidious, because it takes a bit of reflection to realise what's going on – or not going on, to be more precise. It's one of the subtle characteristics that differentiates cultures. A Dutch government official told me that she had the same experience when moving from Limburg province to The Hague. So it's not just Brussels.

In fact, eye contact, like gestural language, is one of the behavioural traits that divides cultures profoundly. Whereas Anglo-Saxons think that not looking one in the eye is a sign of shiftiness (which is often untrue in any case), many peoples from other countries and continents find sustained eye contact unduly intrusive or even offensive. Early on I had the experience of a group of African youngsters looking steadfastly at their feet as I was talking to them. What I at first thought was a mark of disrespect turned out to be the opposite.

It is a reality that people from different cultures often use their eyes differently when communicating. Brits and Americans are inclined to look at someone when he or she is talking to them, partly out of respect, but will tend to look about them more when doing the talking. Some Nordics, in contrast, will often look away when being talked to, but will tend to look fixedly at their audience when talking. This raises the intriguing prospect of a conversation between a Brit and a Swede where neither looks at the other at the same time...

Anyway in Brussels, in the late-1960s, it was virtually impossible to get even a hint of an exchange – unspoken or other – with the average man-in-the-street. A rather startling exception was the woman on the Boulevard Anspach whom I overheard challenging her male tormenter with the words "I'm not a whore because I'm the owner of a four-storey building" *("Je ne suis pas putain puisque je suis propriétaire d'un immeuble de quatre étages, figurez-vous!")*. That seemed to prove Trotsky's point: real estate rated higher than personal morality in the Belgian value system.

But Belgium has seen significant changes for the better on both fronts in recent years. Belgian pragmatism (call it opportunism, if you will) has helped this country pioneer major developments like the new Antwerp docks, the motorways, the TGV network – developments that would have taken ten times as long to realise in Germany or Holland.

Now, after more time here than I care to admit, I guess I've got used to the place. When I arrived, Brussels was still a hesitant claimant to the title of capital of Europe. Now, although no one is prepared to admit it officially, it is *de facto* the capital of Europe. Also Belgium always was historically, and still is, at the heart of Europe. With the accession of Austria, Finland and Sweden in 1995 it also found itself - albeit temporarily before the latest wave of newcomers - geographically at the centre of the European Union. The exact spot was *Le Trou du Diable* at Oignies-en-Thiérache, a cosy little Walloon backwater just north of the French frontier.

They say that, if you manage to stick out the first five years as a newcomer to Belgium, you're stuck for life. I know lots of Americans, and even some Brits, that have decided that there's no place like Belgium.

One of the reasons is quite simply the 'manageability' of Brussels, compared with Europe's other big cities. "It's a delight to stay in a town where you have all the facilities of a big city without having to cope with the drawbacks of a metropolis, either in terms of its size or the number of its inhabitants." Such sentiments about Brussels are frequently expressed today, in one form or another, by Americans, Brits and Nordics. But in fact these words were those of a Frenchman, Derival de Gomecourt, 250 years ago...
Plus ça change...

The Top 10 Reasons for being Belgian

1. You get to speak three languages, but none of them intelligibly.

2. If other countries want to fight a war, they will do it in your country.

3. You can brew drinks out of fruit, and still call it beer.

4. You are either
   a. like the Dutch, just less efficient
   b. like the French, just less romantic
   c. like the Germans.

5. Decent fries. Real mayonnaise. Great chocolate. The best beer. Need we say more?

6. No one knows anything about you, except the Dutch and French and they make fun of you.

7. More scandals in a week than any other country in a decade.

8. You can drive like a maniac on the road and nobody cares.

9. All your famous countrymen are imaginary.

10. Face it. It's not really a country, is it?

Source: anonymous, but suspected to be Antipodean.

Excerpted from a very long-winded joke on the top 10 reasons for being whatever, this gives pause for thought. Nobody can argue with Point 5 which, I suspect, is the most heartfelt of all. And I can't disagree with Points 2 and 6. The perpetrator of this joke is indeed well informed but Point 3 is inaccurate: there is beer in most of these fruit-flavoured drinks and, as he (not she, I suspect) admits in Point 5, it's the best! But I strongly disagree with Points 1, 4 and 8.

Point 9 is a calumny. The great crusader Godfroid de Bouillon, the Emperor Charles V, César Franck, Réné Magritte, Paul-Henri Spaak, Georges Simenon, Hergé, Eddy Merckx, Johnny Hallyday are all anything other than imaginary and, according to my records, none of them has been a sex offender – unless you accept Simenon's claim that he slept with 20,000 women. Gambrinus, the royal inventor of beer, is a more shadowy figure but firmly established in legend – and he came from this part of the world too.

For good measure you can add Jaques Rogge, the President of the International Olympic Committee, the filmmaking Dardenne brothers, and a couple of Nobel prizewinners, Christian de Duve and Ilya Prigogine – and, while you're about it, throw in the novelist Françoise Mallet-Joris, the pioneer of the plastics industry Leo Baekeland and one of the inventors of the World Wide Web, Robert Cailliau (appropriately Flemish with a French-sounding name). I would even be prepared to argue that the great Charlemagne was a Belgian, even if this upsets the Germans.

As Philippe Geluck (the French-speaking Le Chat cartoonist with a Flemish-sounding name) said, "for a little country of idiots, we have done some things that are not completely useless!" ("*pour un petit pays de cons, on a produit des trucs qui ne sont pas complètement nuls!*")

As for Point 7, the rest of the world sees Belgium as a scandal-ridden country simply because the foreign media find nothing else to talk about. This is otherwise an essentially pleasant, good-natured, live-and-let-live type of country, so there are sure to be lapses from time to time. As for real scandals, who's talking when the French and others have their own paedophile rings and, more recently, over 7,000 British males were listed for actively indulging in Internet pornography.

And then there all the things that the perpetrator of this joke, whoever he might be, omitted to mention. Moreover, contrary to the claim in Point 10, Belgium is a real country, if only in terms of a remarkable 'sense of place'. For evidence of that, please read on.

Brussels, **Belgium** and Beyond

2. Bunkers and bricks

"Belgium is a country invented by the British to annoy the French"
Charles de Gaulle

Even if de Gaulle put a different and pithily Gallic complexion on the matter, most people would say that Belgium is an accident of other people's history, the bit left over after the Great Powers had carved up the rest of the Continent.

This relatively modest portion of God's Earth - 30,000 km^2 of it - provided the stage for a series of dynastic pageants and an unceasing clash of European cultures over millennia, and was the cockpit for many battles. Today Belgium is a cockpit in the modern sense of the word: a control room of the European Union and a country where the Romance and Germanic languages, and many cultures, meet.

The Kingdom of Belgium only came into existence in 1830, but at least it arrived on the map of Europe before Italy (Count Cavour could have had the Belgians in mind when he said: "Now that we have made Italy let us make the Italians"). In fact the creation of this country had repercussions out of all proportion to its size: rumours spread that the Russian Tsar, alarmed at the revolutionary implications of the bid for independence, planned to despatch his Polish army to Belgium – and this sparked a Russo-Polish war!

Belgium's historical role long prior to this event marks the character of its people even today. At the heart of the Holy Roman Empire in its gestatory centuries, with such enchantingly named monarchs as Pip the Short and Big-Footed Bertha, the two sides of the country (at that time, west and east) went their separate ways for a while as Flanders and Lotharingia before integrating within the Duchy of Burgundy in the 14th century. And then the foreigners started interfering...

When you have had almost every European nation marching through the living room (which someone with a deviant English sense of humour called the *Lebensraum*), it's not surprising that you develop a defensive tick. That's exactly what many Belgians have: a healthy scepticism plus a tendency to batten down the hatches at the slightest sign of trouble, what I call a 'bunker complex'. History has taught them to react to developments rather than to initiate them. Hardly surprising in the circumstances!

I commented on this in my first book, *We Europeans*, when I wrote that a sense of caution, if not alarm, "was evident in the opening days of the Gulf War when many Belgians revealed a deep-set and atavistic siege mentality. Within 24 hours of the outbreak, stocks of many essential products – sugar, pasta, flour, coffee, cooking oil – had disappeared from retailers' shelves. Foreigners were amazed: one woman was seen leaving a supermarket with 70 kilos of washing powder in her trolley."

I should not have been surprised, therefore, when a Belgian café proprietor told me, during the recent Iraq War, that the older folk were no longer coming out to enjoy their traditional day-time – let alone night-time – tipple. The sense of caution in the older generations is very deep-set.

This bunker complex translates in daily life into an apparent suspicion of other people's motives, particularly foreigners' – behaviour that is in stark contrast with the other overriding feature of the Belgian character, an innate humanity. It extends into business: the Swedish manager of a well-known photocopier company told me that, while he could sell his machines to the Dutch on the strength of a catalogue reference, the Belgians expected a week's use of a demonstration model to make up their minds. This suspicion is evident in the problem of selling PCs on-line to the Belgians: Apple, Dell and HP have all had disappointing results.

In his book *Belgian Adventures* Dutch journalist Derk-Jan Eppink talks about a fellow-Dutchman who was running a metal processing company near Mechelen: "In particular, he was having trouble communicating with his staff. 'I've tried to encourage more worker participation', he told me. 'I've said to them all: "my door is always open; if you think there is a better way of doing things, just come and tell me."'" Unfortunately, this openness had met with a zero response. Not a single member of his Flemish staff had been to see him. Worse still, a number of them had actually resigned. 'How is that possible?' he asked me. 'I only meant it for the best.'"

Jon Chambers, a British manager with a major US multinational also operating in the Mechelen area, encountered the same problem but found the right answer: "In Belgium, there is a strong sense of hierarchy and people working for me wouldn't disagree with me or offer their opinions. I realised the Flemish are quite reserved and now I work with this, instead of against it."

This cautious attitude to the rest of the world, which is common to both Flemish and French-speaking Belgians, extends to a reluctance to admit the outsider to family life. Many foreigners who have lived for years in this country have not yet had the distinction of crossing the threshold of a Belgian home: if you're invited for a meal, you're more likely to be invited out. The live-and-let-live spirit of the country may look to outsiders like benign neglect but, at least, the neglect is benign.

It may be because of such inhibitions that, when Belgians receive a personal invitation from foreign residents, they will treat it and them with respect – and perhaps even too much. An Italian colleague who has a lot of experience of such things says his Belgian guests will often arrive early and leave late, expressing in their own way their appreciation of the honour of being invited.

But the defensive tick of many Belgians is evident in the early skirmishes of trying to develop a relationship with them. A German international businesswoman talks of the difficulty of crossing the border between the professional and the private. "I have got to know a number of them quite well in my dealings," she comments, "and they are friendly enough. But if I even try to ask an innocent question touching on their private lives, they are as secretive as the Finns." And that's saying a lot...

Softly, softly, catchee monkey

The Belgians' innate and highly developed spirit of self-defence extends to a reluctance to recommend a business or a job opportunity to a friend – for fear of losing the friend. Maybe this has something to do with the fact that they are a bit more human than most of us: history has certainly taught them to be responsive to circumstances. The leitmotiv of the culture is, in their own words, *"stilletjes aan"* or *"doucement"* ("softly, softly, catchee monkey").

Even getting to know Belgians in the first place is, for many foreigners, an achievement. In the words of Francis Heylighen, a research professor with the Free University of Brussels (VUB) and a contributor to an interesting website *(www.pespmc1.vub.ac.be)*, Belgians "tend to be rather reserved or introverted in their first contacts with other people, but are sincerely warm and friendly once you get to know them better." He's Belgian and he knows his culture well!

But, for foreigners like me and many others, it takes time to find out. A Dutch friend of mine who has lived in the country for thirty years says: "I still don't know whether I like the Belgians or not" (of course, as I explain in Chapter 8, there are no neighbours more different than the Belgians and the Dutch). Americans, by contrast, often feel personally rebuffed by the lack of contact: they don't understand that Belgians place a high value on privacy.

History has also taught the Belgians that what others can't see, they can't covet. Hence the closed shutters - the diametric opposite of life in the Netherlands - and the barrages of aspidistras and bric-a-brac lining many front windows. But these things do not deter the occupants from spying on passers-by. Though they have now mostly been retired from active service, when I first came here I used to marvel at the 'wing mirrors' mounted on the walls of many 19th century town houses in the provincial cities of Flanders.

Maybe their natural caution also has something to do with the fact that the Belgians are balanced on the knife-edge of history, on the fault-line between the Germanic and the Latin peoples who make up the two majority cultures of western Europe. Many Belgians, god bless them, are potential schizophrenics, having to equate within themselves these two essentially different ways of coping with reality.

The more educated ones do this remarkably well and are an object lesson to the rest of us. Others fail to rise to the occasion, taking shelter within the comforting cocoons of their communities. And most of them fail to realise they have something right here under their noses - this bridging of two major cultures - which other Europeans can only envy and which is the key to the Europe of the 21st century.

In fact, for foreigners arriving here and alert to the differences between the two principal Communities - the Flemish and the French-speakers – the biggest surprise is to find that this largely notional distinction between the two sides of the country is dwarfed by the differences within each of these Communities. I speak of the spirit of localism, which I look closer at in Chapter 5.

One other frequent observation by new arrivals in the country is the average Belgian's assertion of his personal rights, most notoriously the motorist's *priorité de droite/ voorrang van rechts* (and how many Belgians are not motorists?). This squares up poorly with the bunker complex: maybe 'my car is my bunker and my freedom,' all at the same time? It's also odd because the rule was only introduced to the country in 1961, yet it is as deeply rooted in the Belgian culture as something that has been around for much longer in this Pays de Cockaigne: good living.

While we're on the subject, driving licences were only introduced in 1967 – and then at first with nothing more than a theoretical classroom test of the new driver's mastery of the *Code de la Route/Verkeersreglement*. 'Old' drivers were granted a licence automatically, a fact that contributed to foreigners' equally deeply rooted belief that Belgians as a group are dangerous drivers.

But, thanks to their commitment to good living and their dedication to consuming vast quantities of red meat, most of these 'old' drivers are now dead. The ones that are left share responsibility for the people's reputation as roadhogs – something that neither the statistics nor my personal experience seem to bear out.

A product of the bunker complex (and a lot of hard work)?

"Discovered in Flanders, a part of western Belgium, along the North Sea, the endive fits right in with a long line of proud Belgian foods. These people are noted for their twice-fried "frites" potatoes, delicious mussels, jumbo waffles, dark, rich chocolate and legendary beers. Their very own Brussels sprouts were "engineered" over 400 years ago.

Belgian endive was the result of an accidental agricultural discovery which produced delicious results. In 1830, the head horticulturist at the Brussels Botanical Gardens, an M. Brezier, neglected some chicory plants set in a dark warehouse, and the plants blanched for lack of light. The resulting pale, whitish-yellowish, four to six-inch cones of petals surfaced as a delicious new vegetable. Thirty more years went by before Belgian endive was ready for the open market. Almost immediately after it was introduced into Paris' haute cuisine, the French declared it "white gold."

To make the new veggie market-ready, growers had to duplicate the "accidental discovery" and work with the double-growth process. First, they planted plain endive and let it grow a tap root with a crown of green, ragged leaves. They harvested these roots, trimmed the leaves off then replanted them indoors in the dark. This forced the growth of tight cones of pale, succulent leaves. Frequently, each cone is wrapped in purple paper to prevent full greening. The basic endive family is a large one. Belgian endive, curly endive, escarole and radicchio are all members of the chicory family of lettuces. Each differs considerably in form, color and to some extent, taste. If grown under proper techniques, most will produce the root frequently used in coffee as a "chicory additive," especially in French/Creole cultures.

Gaining in popularity, Belgian endive is now grown on most every continent. In this country, it's raised in California, while Holland and Belgium supplement our crop. Hydro culture is a method of growing which works well with Belgian endive.

Definitely a dieter's friend, each leaf is only one calorie. It's also an excellent source of calcium, vitamins A, B and C, also folate and potassium. This fancy is also fat, sodium and cholesterol free."

From: *www.foodsiteoftheday.com/belgianendivef.htm*

A brick in the belly

If it is fair to say that an Englishman's home is his castle, then a Belgian's home is his fortress. This is the ultimate refuge for people with so highly developed a bunker complex.

Appreciation of creature comforts starts in the home - aided and abetted by the average Belgian's skills not only as a do-it-yourself expert but also as a housebuilder. Take a Sunday afternoon drive into the provinces and you will see whole families laying bricks or putting the roofs on their new houses. The Swabian dictum of *"Schaffe, schaffe, Häusle baue!"* ("Work hard, work hard, build a little house!") applies with even greater force to many Belgians, the Flemish in particular. And, once they have built their house, they descend in swarms on the nearest furniture warehouse and indulge in a wild frenzy of acquisition.

Every Belgian, as the saying goes, has a brick in his belly. Homes tend to be cosy, overheated and – particularly in Wallonia – overfurnished with excruciating so-called 'Spanish-style' tables, chairs and cupboards. One Belgian salon I had the honour of frequenting was so full of furniture that it was almost impossible to sit down - a self-defeating situation which didn't seem to have occurred to its owners. They obviously never used it for themselves.

At the other extreme, I came across a home which, from what I could see from the outside (not all that much, what with shutters, curtains, etc), was very lavishly appointed with a grand glass chandelier and expensive wall coverings. A fuller inspection showed that this was the sum of the contents. The owners had still not saved up enough money to buy the furniture, but were motivated by the need to put on a good show for the neighbours.

The latter, as I have already indicated, were in any case unlikely to be invited inside unless they were good enough friends to share a secret - including the state of 'concubinage', as it used to be quaintly called here, which is another aspect of the Belgians' taste for the good things in life.

Closely implicated in this appreciation of home life is the Belgians' sense of family. Anglo-Saxon observers comment on the phenomenon of Sundays when, as a matter of almost instinctive ritual, the various generations spend time together. In *The Low Countries* yearbook, fellow-Brit John Mace writes: "In Belgium the family is alive and well: the feeling of belonging to it is very strong, often to the detriment of one's obligations to a broader group or to the community as a whole."

There is indeed not only a strong sense of family but a remarkable ability – remarkable in this day and age - to bridge the generations, without any of the self-consciously hierarchical impulses of many Anglo-Saxons. I had a particularly engrossing example of this when watching a mother and her grown-up son conducting a public demonstration in the street of something called *biodansa*.

There was no sign of embarrassment on either side, whereas most Anglo-Saxon youths in the same situation would have been mortified.

I have also had occasion to see Belgium's children's courts at work. It is a relief to say that they are a shining exception to the arbitrariness and procrastination of the country's main judicial system. The judges and attorneys apply an impressive degree of sympathy, thoughtfulness and human understanding to the often complex issues they are confronted with.

In the typical Belgian family the generations are mutually supportive and cheerfully share their existence, even to the extent of wedded children staying in the parental home for the first years of their marriage. It may help explain why I have rarely, if ever, seen a young Belgian girl with a 'sugar daddy': they have the real thing. Of course, as everywhere else in Europe, the ties are loosening but the Belgian exception is evident.

This admirable sense of family, even if overdone, extends to the wholehearted and totally unselfconscious integration of Third World children, adopted or not, into the home. Provision is also often made for grandparents, either under the same roof or close by: but this does not prevent them from feeling treated like second-class citizens by their nearest and dearest, according to a recent Eurobarometer survey. Maybe the reason not more old folks end up in homes is because these rather dubious institutions - ironically dubbed

Ma Paix, Avondstilte, Tranquillité du Bois and the like - are almost always located on the noisiest traffic intersections, close to railway lines, etc. At least these senior citizens have uninterrupted entertainment as the cars crash and the trains go by.

The Dutch will probably tell you, once again, that these old-fashioned ideas about family are just more proof of the fact that Belgium is at least ten years behind the rest of Europe. But they are, in my opinion, deceiving themselves if they think this is a hangover from a pre-industrial society. The Belgian attitude to family is heavily ingrained and comes quite naturally, despite the occasional sensational case of paedophilia and the occasional rebel.

It has to be added, however, that there are some Belgians who find this sense of family unduly stifling - like the husband who went temporarily off the map when despatched to collect his wife's mother for the ritual Sunday outing (some Belgians share the mother-in-law problems of the Brits). He turned up a few days later suffering, he claimed, from memory loss.

Brussels, **Belgium** and Beyond

3. The surrealist realists

"Ce pays improbable."

Le Monde, 07.03.2005

Contrast and contradiction are the essential flavours of
Belgium and its cultures. This is a surrealist country, where
day-to-day reality challenges the foreigner's powers of
imagination. Moreover, Belgium takes its extravagances
seriously: look at the success of artists like Magritte, Ensor
and Delvaux, the work of Victor Horta and other Art
Nouveau architects, the achievements of generations of
cartoonists like Hergé, even the fantasies of contemporary
landscape architect Jacques Wirtz.

This being Belgium, contradictions are everywhere: nothing
could be more poignantly realistic than the award-winning
films of the Dardenne brothers. Yet, in the words of a
perceptive American friend, "Belgian surrealism is essentially
visual. When it comes to words or ideas, the tendency is to
be too literal."

Belgians do indeed tend to be a rather literal-minded people.
This is a simple observation, not intended as a criticism.
In many aspects of life it makes great sense to be literal-
minded, in others less so. Yet, as the Dutch can tell you,
when confronted with an intellectual impasse Belgians can
be surprisingly creative. In challenging situations they have

a remarkable ability to think 'outside the box'. So the contradiction between surrealism and literal-mindedness may not be so surprising after all.

A book published in 1992, *Tant qu'il y aura des Belges*, encouraged some of the leading lights of the country, French and Dutch-speaking, to enumerate the characteristics they felt their compatriots have in common – the aim being to counter the perceived threat of a break-up of the country. This produced the following contrasty compendium: the Belgian is imaginative yet close to reality, lives in the present but is suspicious of ideas (the French are obviously lurking in the background here!). He/she is a man/woman of action, has lots of energy, says things the way they are, is sociable and a good team player, and is a practical mediator.

"Imaginative yet close to reality"! The singer Pierre Rapsat, another Belgian distinguished in his chosen field of endeavour, said that his compatriots had only two natural advantages: their geographical position and their powers of imagination...

Francis Heylighen acknowledges that the Belgian reality is "very complex and counter-intuitive for people living in different types of culture." Which is another way of saying that, quite often, we foreigners just don't get it (consider the drawn-out joke in the introduction to the previous chapter).

Another contrast is the varying landscapes of the country itself, arguably Europe's best-kept tourist secret. Belgium is extraordinarily beautiful in a very unpretentious way. One feels a historical symbiosis between the people and the land. Even the old buildings – farms, castles, manor houses – look as if they have grown organically from the ground that supports and surrounds them.

The landscape of Belgium extends from the *polderland* of Flanders with its jewel-like mediaeval towns, through the *Pajottenland* to Brussels, onwards to the Ice Age landscape of the *Fagnes/Venen* in the east, the heathlands of the *Kempen/Campine* in the north and, southwards, to the exquisite valley of the Meuse (more than a match for the Rhine), the sweeping uplands of the Ardennes... with much more in between.

This rich variety of landscapes in such a small space is matched by the variety of cultures. No country in western Europe can match Belgium for its spirit of localism – what some would call the 'parish pump syndrome' (for more on this, see Chapter 5). Yet, contrariwise, Belgians – with notable exceptions – can show great open-mindedness and tolerance of others. History has in effect taught them to cohabit with foreigners.

Everyday Belgian life is also full of contradictions, occasionally spilling over into the realms of absurdity, as some of the almost kafkaesque scenes related on the inside pages of the daily papers confirm.

One of my earliest and fondest recollections is the press report of a wife and her lover, tucked away somewhere in a hamlet on the banks of the Meuse, who engineered a plot to rid themselves of a superfluous husband. The idea was to get him blind drunk and stifle him with a pillow, so that the result looked like an innocent case of cardiac arrest. The first part was easy but, the husband being a robust and muscular man, the second part proved unrealistic. The husband emerged from the experience the following day with a massive headache and a faint suspicion that something had happened that had definitely not been on his agenda...

The fact that Belgians, like many of us, are a sublimely bastard race has helped ensure the contrasts. The evidence is to hand, for example, in people's surnames. Much to the consternation of others – and of myself, when I get it wrong – I still tend to assume that anyone with a name like Vanderstappen, Paelinck or Willems is a French-speaker and anyone with a name like Leroy or Montaigne speaks Flemish (I have plenty of examples to go from). Only recently I found myself talking to a retired crime inspector from the Flemish city of Kortrijk: he not only had the extremely French-sounding name of Jean-Marie Bernard but, in the best Belgian tradition, demonstrated a sense of humour that you don't expect from someone who, professionally, has to take himself so seriously!

What do you do with a country where Flemish party activists have names like Bert Anciaux, Leo Delcroix, Yves Leterme and Geert Bourgeois (at least the Geert sounds authentic)? The burgomaster of the very Flemish commune of Putte at the time of writing is a Heer Bouderie, and the current leader of the French-speaking Walloon Region is Van Cauwenberghe. As I said in the previous chapter, the co-founder of the World Wide Web (another example of a Belgian who should be famous, but isn't) is a Robert Cailliau – and it turns out that, despite his very French-sounding name, he's Flemish.

The reality is that there are no rules and the result is, once again, surreal.

Anarchists at heart

The surrealism of the country certainly owes something to the law-defying character of the average Belgian. Thomas Owen (real name Gérald Bertot), the Belgian crime writer and master of the fantastic, says that "surrealism is a superior form of sedition." The Belgians are certainly seditious... Given the country's history, this is hardly surprising. Dutch journalist Derk-Jan Eppink, who has made Belgium his home, says: "When you have been used to dodging Spanish laws, Austrian laws, French laws, Dutch laws and most recently German laws, it is only to be expected that people will continue to try and dodge Flemish laws and Belgian laws. Particularly as most Belgians still regard the Belgian central government as a form of foreign occupation!" Not to mention European laws...

The British historian Patricia Carson, who lives in this country, clarifies attitudes when she says that the Belgian "avoids, if humanly possible, contact with authority. This applies just as much to the police as to the tax collector. Whenever and wherever the Belgian can outwit authority, he is honour bound to do so."

Francis Heylighen paints an even broader brush: "Belgians instinctively distrust any system that tells them how they should think, behave or produce art." The historian Georges-Henri Dumont maintains it was the influence of the French occupation of 1794-1814 that encouraged what he sees as an "almost visceral resistance to excessive centralisation."

A German journalist and author, Marion Schmitz-Reiners, sums up the essential disposition underlying these attitudes in a few pointed words. Having been married to a Belgian and having lived in Belgium for many years, she says: "The Belgian defers to any authority yet, in his heart, he is a convinced anarchist." I cannot think of any description that fits him or her better (particularly him)!

Being a convinced hedonist as well makes it easier to bend the rules. Parklands and ponds around Brussels are littered with signs saying 'keep off the grass' (or, in winter, 'keep off the ice'), but this doesn't prevent ordinary people from enjoying themselves. A large hole in the *Place Flageyplein* was recently temporarily filled in with sand and surrounded with signs declaring *acces interdit – verboden toegang*, but in no time at all the combination of sun and sand prompted a game of petanque...

If Belgians are nature's anarchists, then it follows that Belgian society starts from the lowest common denominator, the individual. The role model - well known to most foreigners, whether they have lived in Belgium or not - is Till Eulenspiegel (to use the original mediaeval German spelling). Though his role model was a German creation, he was made internationally famous by Belgian author Charles De Coster, appropriately himself the result of a union between a Walloon mother and a Flemish father.

This individualism means that you never know what to expect, not just from the average Belgian (there are lots of them), but also from people in various positions of authority. My personal experience of the humanely anarchic nature of the world of officialdom – witness my exchange with the man who issued my first identity card – is a common experience.

Only recently I found myself interviewing a senior federal administrator for a press feature. I told him about the comment made by a fellow-Brit featured at the head of Chapter 11, viz "The problem with the Belgians is that they can't tell the difference between tax avoidance and tax evasion" and asked him if he objected to my repeating it in print. His response was a typical example of Belgian pragmatism: "As the words are a comment of your experience, I have no problem with them."

Such pragmatism is also evident in many aspects of everyday life. When, in a moment of frustration, I ignored a traffic light as it was turning to red, the policeman on point duty read me the riot act but, then, witnessing my evident frustration and stammered rendering of his Flemish mother-tongue, took pity on me and let me off with a warning.

On another occasion, prompted by the desire to examine one of Wallonia's fabled barge-lifts, I drove along a canal towpath blissfully unaware of the fact that such things are reserved for pedestrians and cyclists. Accosted by a canal official, I commented that it made sense that I take a look at the purpose of my journey, since I was already there. This appealed to the man's sense of pragmatism, so he said "OK, but don't take too long." None of the officiousness of a petty British official with a pip (or a chip?) on his or her shoulder...

A young Belgian I know had a skinful, drove into a tree at high speed and emerged with a broken arm. The patrol man on the scene checked that the lad was out of danger, that nobody else had been hurt and that the car was fully covered for insurance, then said: "OK, I'm not going to report the fact that you were drunk. Nobody else is going to be the worse for that."

The individualistic trait of the Belgians is powerful, but it does not override their basic human instincts. They will judge the situation according to the circumstances – and fellow-feeling will often be the final arbitrator.

Their pragmatism can be a powerful attribute in moments of emergency. A British friend who is an insulin-dependent diabetic was on his own at home when he slipped into a coma. An alert caller realised what was happening from his mumblings on the phone and alerted the emergency services. The team got access to the property next door, climbed the garden wall, entered our friend's house through a small back window, and opened the front door to the medics who were at the ready with oxygen and a drip.

The whole operation took some 20 minutes from the first call to the ambulance taking our friend to hospital. The police, the paramedics and the emergency team all spoke English...

This and similar experiences testify to the realism and charitableness that complement the typically Belgian traits of anarchism and opportunism that are evident to most foreigners. "The virtues of the Belgians are practicality and tolerance," says one British observer; "but," he adds significantly, "the individual virtues are much greater than the collective ones." As a resident of a Flemish suburb just south of Brussels – where, in his view, local officials can be mean-spirited, even racist – he says this with feeling.

In their personal relations, when they are confronted with distraught foreigners who have obviously got out of their depth, all Belgians – regardless of Community or conviction – are inclined to be polite and tolerant, in distinct contrast to neighbouring cultures and countries. The least charitable explanation of this may be their pragmatic and uncomplicated way of dealing with things.

The Belgians have a talent for improvisation, often an expression of commonsense humanity. In an article in *The Low Countries* yearbook, fellow-Brit John Mace talks about "the famous muddling through, for which they have their own terminology: *plantrekkerij/tirer son plan.*"

A German visitor, Rudolf Boehm, recounts his introduction to Belgian bureaucracy in another edition of the yearbook: "I had arrived in Belgium on a three-month visit, with no residence permit, no work permit, no health insurance, nothing... So I had to report to the authorities in Korbeek-Lo, the village near Leuven where I was living at the time. At the town hall they told me 'The burgomaster is in his fields' and showed me how to get there. The burgomaster was busy ploughing, and signalled that he would be with me in a minute. I decided to tell him the truth. And in French quite as bad as mine [Boehm did not speak Dutch at the time] he said: *Tout celà est très bien, mon fils, mais on ne va pas raconter celà aux autorités, on n'aura que des ennuis* ('That's all very well and good, my son, but don't go telling the authorities that, you'll have nothing but trouble.').

It is no doubt this visceral dislike of officialdom that helps explain the remarkable – and often unrecognised – record of ordinary Belgians in defying the efforts of their Nazi masters to round up Jewish refugees during WWII. There are countless stories of individual bravery, another factor that demonstrates that Belgians are far more human than they often given credit for by foreigners. Some people like to suggest that the pogrom largely failed because the Belgian communal administrations were so much more poorly organised than their Dutch equivalents, but I think there's more to it than that!

Closely linked to the spirit of anarchism is a sense of opportunism that emulates that of the Italians. The Belgian ex-inmate of a German prisoner-of-war camp in WWII told me that he was one of 3,500 prisoners, of whom about 3,000 were French, 350 Belgian, 100 British and the remaining 50 of various nationalities. Within a few weeks of confinement, this social microcosm had generated its own section leaders and barrack-room heads, as in any prison camp at the time. Of the 142 more or less self-appointed bosses who emerged in this case, 115 of them were Belgian.

In fact this sense of pragmatic opportunism has earned the Belgians, all of them, the soubriquet of 'the Italians of western Europe': there are, of course, a lot of people of Italian descent in places like Liège, Charleroi and the Borinage. But the Belgians have to share this honour with the Danes ('the Italians of northern Europe') and the Poles ('the Italians of central Europe').

This entrepreneurial spirit is evident in many aspects of Belgian business life. Not long ago the Indian IT manager of a major global corporation told me that he had subcontracted parallel projects to German, British and Belgian suppliers. The first two proved infuriatingly bureaucratic and officious in their reactions to his demands, while the Belgian supplier improvised and came up with the goods.

I have even come across a Belgian carpet manufacturer who hit on the idea of trimming his 'offcuts' (the bits left over from the production line), fitting them with compasses so that they could be easily aligned with Mecca, and selling them as personalised prayer mats to Muslims.

The most evident current expression of this Belgian sense of opportunism is the acts of intelligent anticipation that have made Brussels the administrative capital of Europe. We have witnessed a series of rather speculative projects, successful ones like the construction of the European Parliament building, and unsuccessful ones like the proposal to build an HQ for a European defence force in nearby Tervuren.

Belgians are, as a result of their historical conditioning, great masters of the art of compromise. Where the French still say *"c'est impossible!"* French-speaking Belgians will these days say *"pas de problème!"* Where the Dutch say *"onmogelijk!"* or, at best *"gedogen"* (tolerated), Dutch-speaking Belgians will say *"geen probleem!"* And when Belgians do say *"onmogelijk!"* or *"c'est impossible!"*, they will often still do it in any case...

Dutch business people are taken aback at the inventiveness of Belgians when confronted with an apparently impossible situation that demands some kind of negotiated solution. Of course the Dutch have been heard to say that anyone who could stomach the Spanish Inquisition would be capable of anything! A study undertaken in 1993 by Rotterdam's Erasmus University concluded that Belgian entrepreneurs as a whole dislike risk-taking and cultivate compromise "with conservatism." But the same study found that the Belgian need to find a solution, regardless of the logic of the arguments involved, could indeed encourage "creative results."

Devoid of a talent for compromise, the Belgian federal state would no longer exist. In 2005 legislators huddled together to find a solution to the vexed Brussels-Halle-Vilvoorde question, an issue that mixes language zones with voting rights in a typical witches' brew. For once even the Belgians couldn't find a solution to satisfy both sides. So the government demanded a vote of confidence, shelving the issue until the next legislative session. This was the ultimate in Belgian compromise: simply, for once, doing nothing at all.

That is one of the lessons of what is called 'principled negotiation': if you can't find an answer reconciling different viewpoints, set the issue temporarily on one side and, when you come back to it, you may find it's no longer there. But the BHV issue certainly will be...

Anarchic architecture

There is no better evidence of the essentially anarchic nature of Belgium than the country's architecture. Anyone searching for evidence of the visual exuberance, extending to sheer surrealism, of the Belgians – in stark contrast to their everyday literal-mindedness – need look no further than the houses on the streets of Brussels and many other towns.

In the 19th century the sober but beautifully harmonious Flemish-style brick environment of the Brussels of the late Middle Ages gave way to – in fact, was swept aside by - the often pretentiously self-assertive homes of the newly emerging and mainly French-speaking bourgeoisie. Today many Brussels uptown streets are a jumble of nondescript architecture, like a storefront of goods clamouring for the attention of the passer-by. Collectively these houses tend to be a nightmare, but individually many of them are a delight, although some of them still seem to come straight out of Gotham City.

The trick is to go round the back: many of these pretentious facades conceal the most intimate and unassuming of gardens, full of secret places and sometimes unexpected evidence of relatively wild life. Until not long ago there was a chicken run with a noisy rooster in the middle of the *Ilôt Sacré*. Even so there are moments when I yearn for the harmony of London's squares.

Most of these homes were architect-designed by order. This is curious considering the lack of planning control in many areas of Belgian urban and industrial development. This shortcoming is evident not only in the very belated introduction to Belgium of environmental controls, but also in the startling juxtaposition of architectural incongruities. Clearly supervision was restricted to the appearance of individual buildings, with no thought given to the compatibility of one house with its neighbours: hence the juxtaposition of multi-storey blocks and two-storey town houses, and the jostling together of neo-Gothic, Art Nouveau, Flemish traditional, Bauhaus, and lots more.

I have come across old churches huddled within the perimeters of petrochemical complexes, high-rise buildings overshadowing mediaeval monuments, oases of green fields and farmsteads tucked away between office blocks,

Exotic Brussels

Drive around what is generally known as the Rond-Point Moliere (but which is, in fact, graced with the more romantic name of Place Guy d'Arezzo) and you will see a couple of high-tension poles with masses of twigs on top of them. Look closer and you will see they are parakeets' nests. You can see and, even more, hear the parakeets coming and going.

This real-life scenario sums up Brussels: an exotic foreign community looking to a practical Belgian infrastructure for support. Brussels provides a technically neutral environment for those that nest here, wherever they come from.

In the case of the parakeets – they are Indian collared parakeets, I believe – the temperate climate helps. The Ixelles-Elsene ponds are home to Egyptian geese, herons, terrapins and cormorants, and there is even a colony of Siberian chipmunks in the Forêt de Soignes (18,000 of them at the last estimate)!

The parakeets and the high-tension poles demonstrate the interdependence but separate existence of the foreign and local communities. The parakeets depend on the poles. The poles do not depend on the parakeets, but they gain something by their presence.

In the same way Brussels benefits from the presence of such exotic forms of life as the European Community institutions (some of us would class them as banal rather than exotic), international organisations and multinational corporations. And there is not much symbiosis between Brussels and its exotica: they come into contact with one another, they tolerate one another, they are beneficial to one another, but that's it.

This situation is hardly surprising. History has taught the Belgians to live with foreigners as if they weren't there: even the Magyars managed to spend a few weeks in the country during their 10th century round trip of western Europe. Harsh experience has taught the Belgians to make the best of a bad thing, both comfort-wise and commercially.

In fact the Belgians that most foreigners come into contact with (and often complain about) are members of a gentrified Brussels bourgeoisie that has no particular reason to open its doors to them in any case. But, then, all upwardly mobile communities are like that.

This is in contrast to some of the relationships struck up by the foreign exotica with grassroots Belgians, both Flemings (to use a rather old-fashioned word) and Walloons (a rather odd-sounding one). There are still people in this self-effacing country who are proud of their origins in a very quiet way, and are happy to share their culture. Here the relationship is as symbiotic as it is supportive.

But, as the putative centre of the European Community, Belgium is a bit of a disappointment. With many Europeans going at top speed for total synthesis (an unrealistic dream, as recent events have shown), the country seems at times to be going into reverse.

History has, at least temporarily, put us on a tightrope between the European ideal and a return to our roots. Both will certainly survive – but, such being the case, the parish pump mentality seems a bit out of place.

To many foreigners Belgian Community politics look curiously old-fashioned. The Flemish certainly have nothing to worry about: their culture is distinct and tangible enough to resist eradication. Walloon culture is more difficult to define but, even so, distinct. Neither community has to protect its language to the extent of the Bretons or the Basques, for example, because both French and Dutch are shared with bigger neighbours.

It's easy to blame it on the politicians. But as intelligent, pragmatic and generally forbearing people, the Belgians should challenge the irrelevancies. The ultimate idiocy for a foreigner – and something that definitely should not happen in the capital of Europe – is to drive down the avenue Brugmann to Drogenbos and find a signpost pointing to the motorway marked Parijs, Bergen (Mons, in case you didn't know), Charleroi (OK), Namen (Namur) and Rijsel (Lille, believe it or not). At such moments it is a relief not to be a Frenchman or a Norwegian trying to get home for the first time.

The avenue Brugmann, like the Place Guy d'Arezzo, lies at the heart of Uccle/Ukkel or Ukkel/Uccle (depending on your linguistic preference). A well-meaningBrussels resident set his heart on saving a venerable tree in the commune by having it officially protected with the help of an ecological trust with *francophone* roots. This initiative ran up against stern opposition from the Flemish minority, so a second tree had to be designated and sponsored by a *néerlandophone* organisation. The result is that Uccle/Ukkel now has a French-speaking tree and a Dutch-speaking one. Vive l'Europe Unie!

Microscopically, you can explain things but, macro-scopically, you need a sense of humour. Humour is something the Belgians have in good measure but don't use often enough. An attempt to take themselves less seriously, while showing a better appreciation of their own worth, would be welcome.

A supremely sensible people at heart, they have as firm a claim as anyone or anything – including the poles that hold up the parakeets' nests – to be a "central support" for Europe.

Romanesque chapels nestling under massive radar dishes, even a furniture showroom in the middle of a farmyard and surrounded by a residential estate of bijou bungalows.

In the case of the capital, this process has led to the emergence of a new word in the French, English and German vocabularies. "Brusselisation", coined by Germany's *Frankfurter Allgemeine Zeitung* newspaper, refers to the haphazard destruction and redevelopment of a city.

The fact is that generally in this crowded little country, when a site comes on the market, Belgians' real estate reflexes go on 'red alert'.

One of the most disturbing things for people who respect the architectural heritage is the evidence of what French speakers call *le chantage au cancre*: dereliction blackmail. Buildings are deliberately left to rot, windows open to the sky, so that their owners can have them demolished and replaced by more lucrative new developments.

As David Stephens, the founder of the *Pétitions-Patrimoine* association, points out, they are relying on the inertia of the authorities, hamstrung by lack of funds and administrative red tape, and the gridlock of the communal system. In his own words, "heritage protection is far from being a political priority in Brussels. Indeed, if anything, it is regarded as a nuisance, hindering the trade-off of interests which is the normal course of Belgian politics."

It has even led to a typically Belgian compromise solution to the challenges of heritage protection: physically removing an offending building from its site and dumping it somewhere else. This applies to a number of churches and gate lodges in the Brussels region! Another early compromise, even in terms of the belated Belgian art of town planning, was the decision by the Brussels council to annex the area along both sides of the uptown Avenue Louise because the communes of St Gilles and Ixelles couldn't afford the upkeep. In terms of both geography and postal districts it's a nonsense, but circumstances dictated - and the pragmatic Belgians found a solution.

Fortunately there are signs that, despite the nonchalance of many communal and other administrations, respect for Belgium's architectural heritage is starting to take hold. The Dutch may be right when they say that things happen later in Belgium, though that is no reason for them to feel self-righteous. The most recent evidence of Belgian time-lag is the reluctant recognition of the crowd-pulling potential of industrial archaeology - something that Belgium, thanks to its role in the Industrial Revolution, has in abundance.

It was in fact a Frenchman, Maréchal de Villeroy, who prompted the first and, until recently, only act of Belgian architectural conservation. Arriving on the southern outskirts of the city in 1695 during the Thirty Years War (one war before the one that Marlborough distinguished himself in), he trained his cannon on the spire of Brussels' town hall and flattened the Grand'Place and surrounding area, though surprisingly leaving the spire intact. In an unprecedented spirit of enlightenment and precocious foresight, the city authorities imposed a system of building permits and subjected all reconstruction work to strict specifications.

Maybe as an act of contrition for this untypical development, two centuries later Brussels' masters demolished a whole block of elegant Flemish brick buildings between the Grand-Place and the Place Royale to make way for the monstrous Mont des Arts. The country's architects, too, have managed to impose some intriguingly ugly creations on the landscape, particularly neo-gothic and byzantine churches. One example is the Royal Chapel at Laeken which looks like the creation of a deranged mechanical engineer, a set of oil prospectors' drills turned upside down.

Lack of concern for the environment (and for onlookers' eyes) is equally evident in the provinces. John Mace talks of "a reckless ribbon development in which harmony, style and communal responsibility have been sacrificed to individualism." Either that or the opposite where, apparently for taxation reasons, you find houses with a front and a back but, so to speak, no sides: the remarkable thing is that, unlike the serried terraced houses of northern England, these often turn up in the middle of fields and, far from being serried, stand emphatically apart from one another – like slices of slab cake with alternative slices missing.

Despite all of this, compared with their neighbours to the south the Belgians do have some respect for their natural environment. They wouldn't allow the kind of eyesore that is commonplace in northern France. Travel down the Viroin valley to the French town of Givet and the scene changes abruptly from a mellow, beautifully tended landscape on the Belgian side to one of whitewashed kerbstones and weed-infested fields lined with corrugated iron fences.

Maybe this has something to do with the fact that the Belgians extend to nature the live-and-let-live attitude that they apply to neighbours and to visitors. They leave it alone - even tend it respectfully, if they think it will reward them in the long term - unless they have other plans for it. Maybe it also has something to do with the fact that nature in Belgium is extremely beautiful: not just the Flemish polderland or the breathtaking vistas of the Ardennes, but the intimately undulating countryside around the capital.

The most remarkable thing is the exuberance, almost bravado, of the trees in the central province of Brabant. Of a softer green than the trees of my home country and twice as large, they benefit hugely from the combination of a mild, moist atmosphere and the sandy soil. Unfortunately, because of the latter, some of them have a habit of falling over. Equally striking is the luminous green of the catalpas and the tulip trees and, in the early spring, the carpets of speedwell that turn the lawns blue. Other regular features of the environment are the magpies, handed down from the days and paintings of Pieter Bruegel the Elder, and of course the Indian parakeets and the Siberian chipmunks.

In many of its aspects – nature, buildings, the mentality of its people – Belgium is a very mellow country. If you have never known it, it is difficult to imagine the soft, warm and enveloping experience of a Belgian summer or autumn evening.

You might think that Keats would have found his inspiration for 'Ode to Autumn' in this part of the world, if he had actually been here. Contrary to one of the many myths about Belgium, even the weather is gentle. Though the average annual rainfall is higher than the UK, you hardly ever notice it - a soft continental mist contrasting with the emphatic Atlantic downpour that interrupts life every now and then in the British Isles.

4. Divisions and common factors

"Il y a en Belgique, des Wallons et des Flamands;
il n'y a pas de Belges."

Jules Destrée

Having made this politically inspired but otherwise
unhelpful assertion in his famous 'Letter' to King Albert I,
the politician described as 'The Waker-Up of Wallonia' (it
sounds more elegant in French) back-pedalled by admitting
that he was exaggerating.

Was he? There are a lot of Belgians who think not.

What are the differences between the linguistically and
politically opposed communities of Flemish and Walloons?
Destrée again: *"... le Flamand est lent, patient, discipliné autant*
que le Wallon est léger, inconstant et indomptable."

It takes courage to say things like that, even if they were
said nearly a century ago, long before the present scourge
of political correctness. People saw nothing wrong with
stereotypes in those days!

But it would be foolish to imagine that all the members of
any cultural community, region country, whatever, can be
expected to act according to (stereo)type. People, after all,

are individuals: each one of us is unique. Yet I would venture to suggest that there are certain characteristics that would be recognisable in a substantial minority, or even a slight majority, of any social grouping.

Professor Jean Ladrière of the UCL got closer to the truth about the Belgians when he said: "I think the Flemish population of this country has a very strong sense of community... The Walloons had to become aware of the fact that they too are a community." They still have to – and it isn't easy...

The Flemish not only have a very strong sense of community, they also have a sense of historical continuity. And yet, for a people who pride themselves on their common culture and identity, as individuals they manage to be delightfully diverse. At one extreme you have ruddy-faced beer drinkers with a disarmingly simple approach to life, on the other you have potential ascetics – with their sallow complexions and their Mennonite-like beards – who also still manage to fit the creature comforts into their value systems. A rather surprising aspect of Flemish society is a subculture of university professors who, untypically for their kind in any other country, behave like characters from the Wild West, outgoing, extravagant, very funny and sometimes absolutely mad.

Flemish men – like the rest of us – come in all shapes and sizes, and many of them display a simple bonhomie and amiable native cunning that would be worthy of the Good Soldier Schwejk. But from casual observation I conclude that on the distaff side, if one excludes the older generations, there are two starkly divergent groups: Flemish women tend to be either trim and tightly buttoned up, often with a spartanly short-back-and-sides, or luxuriously glossy and groomed.

To Anglo-Saxon ears, spoken Flemish has a mediaeval ring to it and Flemish voices can sound decidedly old-fashioned: yet they also offer infinite variety. For a start, the Flemish speak a much more agreeable version of Dutch than the Dutch, who will admit this themselves. Some Flemish women have very mellifluous voices with a remarkable range of tone and expression. Yet there are newscasters and commentators on Flemish TV and radio, female and male, who talk like morticians (a melodious exception is the man who introduces the morning programme on Radio Klara). There are others who talk, rather unconvincingly, like disk-jockeys: they manage a staccato style with a crackle of consonants that couldn't be bettered with castanets. Both species roll their r's with great enthusiasm.

The ultimate irony is that, common culture notwithstanding, some Flemish people have great difficulty in understanding one another: when a Limburger talks to a Westvlaming, despite the relatively modest distance, it's like a Scotsman trying to communicate with a man from Mousehole. But more of that in Chapter 5.

In temperament, the Flemish also have their extremes, from the exceedingly amiable to the excessively severe. For British people, they can seem slightly brusque but encouragingly businesslike, and essentially very good-natured. Some of them can be indefatigably jolly. If you want to see how even elderly provincial Flemings can live, go to the 'Orient-Express' café in Lier, next to the Timmertoren clock, and look around you: this will be enough to convince you that they are not as straight-laced and buttoned up as we may think or as they may appear – but, then, that's Lier. The town is worth a visit in any case. It's as pretty as Bruges and there are a lot less tourists.

Yet there is still a prim and proper side to Flemish provincial life that helps explain the tendency of more and more youngsters to move into Brussels in order to be able to breathe freely. With their relatively recent rise to prosperity, Flemish people tend to be more status-conscious than most Walloons: larger houses, larger cars and the like. And yet, if you wander around the Flemish countryside, you will see plenty of evidence of the commonsense compromise you can expect of any self-respecting Belgian: your typical bijou freestanding residence is just as likely to have chickens, rabbits and goats in the backyard and the master's monster articulated lorry (a lot of Flemish males prefer self-employment, in this case working as truckers) in the front.

In business, the Flemish show a marked degree of application and commitment. They are industrious, serious-minded under the bonhomie, and generally trustworthy. Their conviction that they have been short-served by history, and particularly by the French-speaking bourgeoisie, gives them a great sense of common purpose that Flemish politicians exploit shamelessly and that they themselves put to good use by networking furiously within their own community. Most of the time they are emphatic in their opinions – but this doesn't stop them from keeping their opinions to themselves, in the time-honoured Belgian way, when the circumstances demand it.

Educated Flemish people easily transcend the Dutch-French language barrier (and others as well), even if they are sometimes reluctant to do so, and they have an admirable ability for encompassing the Latin culture as well as their own – a skill that is out of reach of many of the other Germanic peoples. In fact, when the move to champion the Dutch language in its own right got under way in Flanders, much of the opposition came from the Flemish bourgeois elite - many of whom were, inevitably at the time, French speakers.

Yet the present urge to align in opposition to the French culture has the consequence that, despite their basic fair-mindedness, the Flemish often don't bother to make the distinction between the French-speaking and French-aping elite of Brussels and some of the bigger Flemish cities, and *les Wallons des bas-fonds* – many of whom, as an aside, have Flemish or Frankish blood in any case.
This is unfortunate.

Again, you can blame it on history. "Your average Fleming is not really a political creature, but he has always had a strong feeling for the underdog," explains Dutch journalist Derk-Jan Eppink. "Throughout their history the Flemish people have been oppressed by foreign invaders and by their own French-speaking elite, so that they know exactly how it feels to be bullied and ignored."

...and the Walloons?

As Jean Ladrière points out, the Flemish have a coherent sense of nationhood – one that sets them apart from both the French speakers of the country and their Protestant Dutch neighbours to the north – but the Walloons lack a single and clear identity. There are strong local cultures focused on the principal towns of Wallonia: Liège, Namur, Charleroi, Mons, Tournai in particular. The people of Luxembourg province feel closer to the Luxembourgers of the Duchy than to anyone else, while many of the people in the Liège area associate with the culture of France.

In fact, the closest to France, in terms of both geography and speech, are the people of Tournai. Most other Walloons have distinctive accents and colloquialisms – which they often use to determine one another's origins – while sharing a tendency to vocalise their vowels with a nasal twist.

If I dare to make a general comment on the Walloon culture, it is that they have a *bon enfant* side that is appealing but at times rather naive. Friendship rather than networking comes first for the relatively laid-back Walloons: I know of a Walloon supervisor whose stress symptoms were eventually traced to his compulsion of going around his department first thing every morning, shaking every member of his team by the hand and investing in small talk. Walloon workers can be evasive, when challenged on issues, but are particularly likely to respond to sympathetic treatment from those in authority.

Of course, the Flemish like to think that the Walloons are somewhat self-indulgent, flaky and speculative, while the Walloons perceive the Flemish as dour, excessively rigorous and unimaginative. A British international businessman claims it is relatively easy "to know where you are with the Flemish" while the Walloons "are more elusive." But the two sides definitely meet in the middle.

A state-of-the-art assessment came to me from a canny Flemish management consultant – ironically someone, once again, with a French-sounding name – who said: "When I send an email to a Walloon, I come straight to the point. But when my Walloon colleague emails back, he starts by asking me how I am and did I have a good weekend?… and then he gets to the point. And I feel angry. And I ask myself, is that because of what the politicians keep on telling me, or is it simply because we are different? But, when I meet my Walloon friend, we get on very well together and we enjoy ourselves."

Yes, there is a difference, but that's what makes Belgium so great. It bridges the two Western European cultures, the Germanic and the Latin. It's a question of emphasis, of which comes first: Who you are? Or, what are we trying to do? The underlying value system is the same.

One point in the middle where the two sides definitely meet is a common sense of fun: both (forget the German-speakers for the moment) enjoy letting their hair down when they can. It's a modest extension of the taste for the good things in life. All self-respecting Belgians love it when the circus comes to town, they delight in stalls and sideshows. And, if they can't get anything better, they will be content with a street market, a *braderij/braderie*. They're like kids, and all the better for it...

I love Flanders for its orderliness and its strong sense of history, punctuated by this repeated surrender to the street culture. I love Wallonia for its spontaneity, its casualness and the bits that are still beautiful. 19th-century industrialisation made a mess of some of the landscapes, but it is still possible to find idyllic spots as little as five kilometres from the industrial scrap-heaps of the Sambre valley.

For me, the real differences are not between the Flemish and the Walloons (and the German speakers for that matter), but between the Flemish... and the Flemish, and the Walloons... and the Walloons. The German-speakers by comparison are a fairly coherent group. But more about that in Chapter 5.

As for the culture of Brussels, comparing my impressions today with my recollections from the late-1960s, I feel that the *gratin de Bruxelles*, the upwardly mobile folk of the capital city, have improved with the passage of the years. Like anyone uprooted and *arriviste*, regardless of nationality, they still have a tendency to take themselves too seriously. Self-absorption can be mingled, rather disconcertingly, with a gentle self-deprecation. At least that's an improvement on the pomposity and self-importance I witnessed on first arriving in Belgium – epitomised in the god-like utterance of a self-made patron who declared, in justification of his autocratic rule, *"J'ai besoin de mediocres"* ("I need mediocre people")!

The aging females of this Brussels tribe often give themselves away with their fluting falsetto voices. By comparison, though depleted in numbers through social advancement and exodus to the suburbs – and swamped by a mass of exotic immigrants – the less fortunate indigenous folk of Brussels still delight foreigners with their outrageously folkloric scruffiness.

A knee-jerk reaction

With some justification many Flemish people seem to have a knee-jerk reaction to relations with their French-speaking neighbours when an inter-Community issue presents itself or a Flemish politician speaks. It's rather like one of those scientific experiments where you take a pile of iron filings and put a current through it: suddenly they all point in the same direction.

This knee-jerk reaction is often only half-conscious, more a ritual than of real import. Francis Heylighen of the VUB asserts that "there have never been any real conflicts between Belgian (Walloon and Flemish) people, as opposed to conflicts between Belgian politicians." So foreigners should not conclude that there is a major undercurrent of ill-will between the two sides. Leaving apart the radical and lunatic fringe, young people – tired of politicians and more absorbed by other issues – seem increasingly to feel the issue is for the birds.

An only superficial knowledge of the history of this part of the world is enough to explain why the Flemish have a grudge. Even before the turn of the 19th century, the main cities of what was to become Belgium witnessed the emergence of a French-speaking bourgeois elite possessing what must have seemed, for many of their Flemish neighbours, a frightfully unnatural set of values and mores. Flemish speakers either became second-class citizens or, as happened with many shop-keeping folk who migrated from Flanders to Brussels to seek their fortunes, turned their backs even more resolutely on their native culture.

Until 1873 Belgian courts conducted their proceedings in French only. Commissioned officers in the Belgian army were expected to speak French and, though regularly debated, there is certainly some truth in the fact that Flemish foot soldiers died in WWI simply because they couldn't understand the orders of their French-speaking officers.

In the second half of the 19th century popular resentment was overtaken by a Flemish cultural revival where writers, teachers and others politicised the issues. These antagonisms were fuelled by the wealth generated in Wallonia by the 19th-century industrial revolution: Flanders, still a largely rural peasant community, was left on the sidelines, rueful and resentful.

After WWII, the wind changed direction. Flanders was the beneficiary of heavy and sustained US industrial investment when Wallonia's industries were going into decline. The Flemish had their act together and their tails up. The pent-up legacy of resentment now entered the mainstream of politics, most notably in the events in Leuven which led to the creation of Louvain-la-Neuve and the barefaced populism, even demagoguery, of the Flemish Community government in the closing years of the last century under Luc Van den Brande.

Flemish revanchism has even been evident in the directional signs on the motorways. Cross the linguistic frontier and the signs on the Walloon side obligingly and intelligently give you the names in both French and Flemish. It's also perhaps significant that, at the time of writing, the official Walloon Internet website includes hyperlinks to Flemish sites, whereas the Flemish one does not...

Maybe the French Community's strategy is working, because the Flemish government has since been back-peddling its policy a bit. There has also been a growing awareness that Flemish bloody-mindedness has unsurprisingly incited a Walloon tit-for-tat. In stark contrast to the advertising slogan *"Trop is jamais te veel!"*(an inspired bit of inter-Communitarianism attributable to, of all things, a French cheese producer), we foreigners think enough is enough.

The inconvenience caused by monolingual motorway signs has now been reluctantly acknowledged by the Flemish

A river runs through it...

There's a little river that rises in the corn and sugarbeet belt of Belgium's Hesbaye region, less than five kilometres south of the linguistic frontier and not far from a Flemish village on the Brussels-Cologne motorway with the intriguing name of Walshoutem.

The river meanders eastwards, passing amiably and apolitically from the French-speaking part of the country to the Flemish-speaking one and then back again. Then, concluding its course flamboyantly with a five-kilometre dash through nature reserves into Dutch Limburg, past the Netherlands' only vineyard, it loses itself in the mighty Meuse (*Maas* in Flemish/Dutch).

This river is hardly any bigger at the end of its modest 60-kilometer journey than it was at the beginning. The only thing that changes is its name. Every now and then it runs up against the linguistic frontier and inherits a different label: Geer in the French-speaking part of the country, Jeker in the Dutch-speaking part.

Yet it manages to create and support an environment, accessible from a network of winding minor roads that brush against it affectionately all along its course. This changes little from one end to the other - water meadows, willows and watercress beds, strung out like pearls on a necklace of villages and farmsteads.

All along its meanderings through Belgium - whether the community it happens to be passing through is Walloon or Flemish, French-speaking or Dutch-speaking - this little river sustains a way of life that is uniquely and distinctively Belgian. It is one of the tenuous threads, both real and symbolic, that help hold this country together.

authorities – but not in a spirit of reciprocity to the Walloons. International business has been complaining about the disruption caused to the best intentions of non-Dutch-speaking truck drivers, who tend to end up in the wrong places or doing the wrong kinds of things. As Belgians, the Flemish are quick to appreciate the downside of a policy which damages their business interests. So deviation and other instructional signs will now display text in English – not French by any stretch of the imagination – but the place names will stay as they are!

The glue that holds it all together

The most formidable obstacle to getting to know and understand the Belgians is that they come in so many different flavours. They vary so much, not just between the three linguistic communities but also from province to province, of which there are nine, and even more from town to town.

Jean-Paul Picha, the cartoonist, goes so far as to suggest that you can only define the Belgian culture by a process of exclusion, i.e. by differentiating it from the cultures of its neighbours, France, Germany, England and (with particular emphasis!) the Netherlands. I attempt to do this in the closing chapters of this book.

André Jaumotte, honorary rector and president of Brussels Free University (ULB), says much the same thing: "It's difficult to define Belgian identity in terms of common characteristics. I think it's easier to define it in terms of the differences," i.e. the differences between the culture of Belgium and those of its neighbours.

Yet I believe that the Belgians, the Flemish and the Walloons, have some very important qualities in common, an overarching value system that distinguishes them clearly from their neighbours. French-speaking sociologists call it *'belgitude'*. My insistence on this point is often greeted with vigorous cries of protest, particularly from the Flemish, but I know I'm right.

Many Belgians don't see the commonalities, but foreigners have the benefit of viewing these things from a more distant standpoint, with the added advantage of being able to benchmark their conclusions against their experience of their home cultures. We can see both the wood and the trees.

An article published jointly by a university professor Alphonse De Waelhens and a literary critic René Micha in 1949 under the title *Du Caractère des Belges* said the following: "Belgium is not an artificial creation; it derives from a reality which, of secondary importance in other nations, provides the basis for its existence and its unity. Belgians have a common destiny, because they have the same way of behaving, of reacting and of expressing themselves: the same complex of characteristics."

These brave words suggest that Belgium is not an accident of history after all. It is based on the reality of a common culture, unlike most other western European nations which are based on frontiers determined by acts of violence or dynastic marriages and take little account of the cultures they contain.

Confirmation of this commonality comes from a series of studies undertaken by sociologist Professor Jan Kerkhofs of Leuven University (KUL). These show that a consensus exists on fundamental values, and that the Flemish and Walloons are closer together in their value judgements than either the Flemish are with the Dutch (see Chapter 8) or the Walloons with the French (Chapter 9).

Another Belgian who sees the commonality of his country's value system is Francis Heylighen: "Though Flemish and Walloon cultures differ in several respects (as could be expected, the Flemish are closer to the more disciplined, Northern European, Germanic culture, and the Walloons

to the more life-enjoying, Mediterranean, Latin culture),
they have more things in common than most are willing
to admit."

Seen from a Flemish standpoint, many Walloons may seem
relaxed, even disorganised: seen from a Walloon standpoint,
many Flemings seem severe. Certainly their macropolitical
preferences diverge: where the Flemish are instinctively
conservative, the Walloons incline to socialism – a disparity
that owes its existence as much as anything to the two
communities' different environments and histories. But
stand back and the commonalities come into focus.

To paraphrase George Bernard Shaw talking about the
Americans and the British ("two nations divided by a
common language"), Belgium is essentially a common
culture divided by language.

This inevitably begs the question of where this common
culture comes from. The word 'Burgundian' is often evoked
in this context – it has even popped up in sociological
research studies - without really offering anything remotely
like an explanation of Belgium today. The historical
Burgundian culture was, after all, a courtly one and had
little to do with the everyday life of people living in this part
of the world at the time. Moreover, the Duchy of Burgundy
encompassed much of today's Netherlands as well – and
there's not much evidence of a Burgundian culture there.
Michael Jackson, the great Beer Hunter and advocate of
Belgium's delicious Trappist brews (a Brit, he's best known
in the USA), suggests that the Burgundian connection is

more sentimental than historical: "Belgium was once part of Burgundy, and honours that memory. In Belgium, to call someone 'a Burgundian' is an admiring term. When the Flemings and Walloons talk of their most robust beers, they call them 'the Burgundies of Belgium'."

'Burgundian' is one way of describing the culture: another, less complimentary one, is the Land of Cockaigne. But that image also finds its origins elsewhere, in Italy it seems, and has little to do with the sensible appreciation of the good things in life that characterises Belgians today.

Common characteristics

Braving all the traps Belgium places in the path of the unwary observer, let me try to capture some of the common characteristics of the Belgian culture (what I say may only apply to 40 per cent of the people, but that still represents a substantial minority).

Anarchism, which I talked about in Chapter 2, is not the only thing the Belgians – be they Flemish, Walloon, German-speaking or whatever – have in common. Let's deal with what I consider to be the unifying force in Belgian society, despite the individualism and the anarchic impulses.

I mean nothing less than the appreciation of the good things life has to offer. The pursuits of today's Belgians may be somewhat milder than the ones Cardinal Granville referred to in a letter to Philip II of Spain when he said: "Nothing can be done because they only think of stuffing themselves, having orgies and thinking bad thoughts" *("Il n'y a rien à faire de bon, parce qu'ils ne pensent qu'à bafrer, à organiser des orgies et mal penser")*. Both Flemish and Walloons are good trencherfolk by definition. And even the German-speakers of the Ostkantone have no inhibitions when it comes to the creature comforts.

The foreign tourist sees the tip of this hedonist iceberg in the gastronomic standards evident in Brussels' *Ilôt Sacré*. But you will find it anywhere you go in this country - even in the *dagsschotel/plat du jour* of the humblest tavern catering for the office workers of any town, many of which would put the creations of an upmarket restaurant in London or Paris to shame.

It is also evident in the enormous popularity of Belgian chocolates and Belgian beers, ranging from mass-produced lager types (of which my favourite is *Maes*, which allegedly owes its quality to the presence of German prisoners-of-war in the brewery end-WWII) to the almost mystical Trappist fermentations of Belgium's abbeys.

From a British standpoint - that of a country which is not renowned for its pastrymaking in any case - the Belgian gastronomic scene is only marred by the performance of its *banketbakkerijen/pâtisseries*, which manage to produce fruit tarts that taste and feel as if they have been mounted on cardboard. The ultimate in teeth-challenging gastronomy is the gingerbread speciality native to Dinant on the river Meuse: you are advised to crack it into small bits with a hammer. But these are rare exceptions to the good fare rule.

Of course, appreciating life to the full involves paying for it, so there's no question that Belgian materialism includes making money. When Leon Trotsky spoke of 'Belgianisation' or "the abandonment of national responsibility in favour of totally commercial values," he should have realised that a sense of 'national responsibility' was likely to be in short supply in any case, given the country's history.

Every Belgian is a law unto him or herself (for simplicity, I will stick to the masculine hereon, unless logic dictates otherwise). Just as he keeps his thoughts to himself – and quietly sabotages the best-laid plans of mice, men, managing directors and government ministers – he acts out his personal interpretation of what is best for him. As Patricia Carson says in her book *The Fair Face of Flanders*, "The Belgian has become used to having to fend for himself when authority is either non-existent or actively hostile."

But this does not mean he is unremittingly selfish. Far from it, Belgians can be very generous. Perhaps they are least generous to themselves, often selling themselves and the country short. Foreign commentators, critics and comics – and not just the French – have encouraged Belgians to be self-effacing, a tendency that happily seems to be to some extent on the wane. If they now show a greater sense of their own value, they still wonder how their country survives.

One of the most telling symptoms of the innate humanity of the Belgians is the quality of the country's TV talk shows (another is the compassion shown by Belgian juries in family-related court cases while, as an example of the collective human spirit, one only has to think back to the White March). Whereas German TV shows tend to be too severe and politico-technical for my taste and British ones too trivial, any discussion on Belgian television reveals unsuspected layers of profundity, intelligence and, above all, human warmth.

This, fortunately, also comes across in everyday life, with the inevitable exceptions. Provided you don't shout at them on the one hand, and don't put on a pathetic show on the other, they will often sense your distress and go out of their way to help you. If it involves doing something to 'beat the system' then they will do it with even greater enthusiasm. This potential for beating the system is an essential ingredient of the Belgian character.

Among other things ordinary Belgians, unlike the British, have little sense of class – which they compensate for with a well-developed sense of locale. The common touchstone is whether one has been a success or not. Signs of solid wealth (maybe a Mercedes-Benz) are to be preferred to ostentation (Rolls-Royces, etc), again in contrast to the UK today.

Irony of ironies, there is another thing that unites the people of this country. As Renée Fox says in her book *In the Belgian Château*, "I have never encountered a society more prone than Belgium inversely to articulate some of its most fundamental values; more obsessively and doubtingly preoccupied with its 'authenticity' and 'reality'; more concerned about its progressive 'disappearance' and ultimate 'survival'; and more constantly surprised by the fact that 'it still exists'. The continual failure of Belgians to recognize that this 'Belgium-in-spite-of-itself' outlook is part of the shared culture they deny possessing has never ceased to amaze me."

Ik wens dat België blijft bestaan. Niet uit vaderlandsliefde of omwille van de vlag. Maar omdat België interessant is als multiculturele en multinationale staat.

(I want Belgium to survive. Not out of patriotism or because of the flag. But because Belgium is interesting as a multicultural and multinational state.)

Walloon journalist Claude Demelenne, quoted in Solidair, the journal of the Belgian Workers' Party

5. The spirit of localism

"Blame it on my roots"

Slogan on T-shirt

Although occupying a space of only 30,000 km^2 (11,500 square miles) and housing barely more than ten million people, Belgium supports no less than six parliaments plus three other legislative bodies. The public – and bemused foreign investors – are confronted with one federal and three regional governments and, at the time of writing, a grand total of 48 ministers. The country also boasts the greatest density per km^2 of cartoonists and art collectors.

There was a moment when the Japanese government discovered to its consternation that there were three Belgian prime ministers on trade missions to their country at the same time. What better way to illustrate the spirit of localism that characterises Belgium!

This spirit of localism is evident in the Brussels telephone directory – try to find someone who lives on the fringe of the city! – and on the Internet. An otherwise useful street location site only works if you already know which *commune* of Brussels the street is in…

When management gurus invoke the principle of 'Think Global, Act Local' they don't realise, in the case of Belgium, what a long and slippery slope they are on when it comes to the 'local' bit! The good folk of many Flemish villages feel intuitively that the people from the next burg are not really the same as them, in short 'foreigners'. Localism runs riot in the Flemish Community (N.B. Community with a big C, the political definition in order to avoid any confusion). In some cases, this sense of localism is tantamount to parochialism – a mentality splendidly and very amusingly portrayed in the 'Samson' Flemish TV series with its self-important burgomaster, sash and all, surrounded by a bunch of delightful busybodies.

One of my first errors on arriving in Belgium was to mistake a resident of Lier for an Antwerpenaar. Lier, a mini-Bruges which is worth an intercontinental roundtrip for a visit, is just 15 kilometres from Antwerp city centre and divided from the Antwerp agglomeration by only a kilometre or so of greenish field. Yet, both physically and culturally, it is another world (it may also help that it is has a very successful football club).

The people of Lier, along with many of their Flemish cousins, claim to find the Antwerpenaars brash and overbearing: the big city has a lot to be proud of, but so does Lier! In fact, this hostility, mild as it is, is another historical hangover in a country which has seen so much history.

Similar enmities, or jealousies, exist between most regions and cities of Flanders. It is difficult to think that the politically fuelled pride of Flemishness will ever entirely extinguish these ultimately rather charming human quirks. Different dialects often reinforce this spirit of localism.

A Flemish friend of mine, born and brought up in a small village just outside Geraardsbergen, summed up the situation rather neatly when talking to an American: "When you're explaining directions to a visitor in the States, you tell them to go some twenty miles south, take the turning due west and then head south again. Here in Belgium, we tell you to go a kilometer, turn left and then turn right..."

Walloons are as conscious of their roots as the Flemish are. Confronted with the need to move house, a good lady from the town of Mons looked at the options and promptly drew up a blacklist of the places she would not go and live in "because the folks there are not like us." This list included just about every town and village within 15 kilometres of Mons. Anything outside the perimeter was 'Indian territory'.

This spirit of localism – something unknown in much of my home country, in particular the Home Counties – is as deeply rooted today as it was 500 years ago. The fierce local loyalties and rivalries that developed were later incorporated in - and perpetuated by - the communal administrative structure established in Napoleonic times. In the words of a perceptive observer, "Belgium is a republic of communes."

You see the effects most dramatically in the vast tailbacks morning and evening on the motorways leading into the principal centres, especially Brussels (and it's not that the Belgian motorway system is underdeveloped!). The average Belgian will happily put up with the pains of commuting for the sake of keeping his roots where they belong. In fact one Dutch observer of the Belgian scene, a long-time resident, maintains that the decision is taken openly, or by persuasion, by the female partner: she wants to be able to visit her mother regularly and go on using her favourite chemist shop...

I know a young Flemish man who claims there are different cultures between streets in his native town of Zonhoven. Yet he is a good example of another Belgian phenomenon. As an antidote to the sometimes stifling nature of traditional life, many Belgians do something starkly different, either as a hobby or as a full-time occupation. In his case, he is an Internet designer and a very successful businessman.

In Belgium's defence it also has to be admitted that, thanks to being small, it was the first country on the European continent to apply the principle of a standard time reckoning, Greenwich Mean Time, across its entire rail network.

... and the spirit of adventure

Here's another Belgian contradiction, well expressed in the words of cartoonist Jean-Paul Picha: "at one and the same time one senses both the universal character of the Belgians and this incredibly local and small side." ("on sent *à la fois le caractère universel du belge, mais aussi ce côté incroyablement local, petit.").* Belgian localism is astonishing when matched against the spirit of adventure that many of them, Flemish and Walloons, show when they get the opportunity.

It would be a mistake to run away with the idea that the Belgians are stay-at-homes or stick-in-the-muds. There is plenty of evidence, historical and contemporary, to show that both Flemish and Walloons are – in the time-honoured tradition of pragmatism and opportunism – quite prepared to uproot themselves when the opportunity offers. Under the leadership of Godfried de Bouillon, Flemish and Walloon foot soldiers went side-by-side into battle in the First Crusade.

This pioneering spirit is evident today in the number of extremely successful multinational executives with Belgian passports. Even more spectacular is the number of Belgian businessmen and others who use their vacation time to pursue their private passions, climbing mountains in the Himalayas or precipices in Patagonia, going 'underground' in Iran, trekking in Central America (echoes of Hergé's 'Tintin'), and so on. Our local bank manager spends his yearly vacations in the mountains of Nepal and Bhutan and our odd-job man, *un bruxellois de pure souche*, has been working in Israel and Peru...

This wanderlust has been around for a long time. For the benefit of British readers, I should point out that the Belgae – one of the tribes that gave its name to the present-day

Belgian state – were already present in England in Caesar's time (the same Caesar who had earlier complimented the mainland Belgae on their bravery). Well established in what would now be Hampshire and Avon, their towns included their capital, *Venta Belgarum* (today's Winchester), *Magnus Portus* (today's Portsmouth) and possibly also Bath.

Much later in 1105, at the invitation of King Henry I of England, Flemish farmers settled in the southern Dyfed area of Wales, cultivating the no-man's-land behind a row of Norman forts that had been built to contain the unruly Welsh.

Two hundred years later, in 1331, Edward III invited Flemish weavers to settle in the eastern counties. Even today, some people speak of East Anglia as 'Flemish England'. Of course the definition 'Flemish weavers' depends on one's interpretation of what was Flemish at the time. Not only did the Duchy of Flanders extend southwards into the Artois province of France; there is also reason to think that the Flemish/Walloon distinction, even within the confines of today's Belgium, was far more permeable than it would appear to be today.

English communities that owed their subsequent prosperity to these newcomers from Belgium included the wool towns of the West Riding of Yorkshire, the city of Norwich, and the little wool towns of Suffolk: Sudbury, Long Melford and Lavenham, famous for its 'worsteds'.

From the early-14th century onwards, artisans from what is now Belgium emigrated in droves to the English counties of

Kent, Surrey and Sussex, including those who moved to the ironworks of the Haslemere area at the invitation of the ultimately ill-fated Charles I. Linen weavers from Kortrijk and West Flanders settled in Canterbury and other Kentish towns, and brought a taste for good beer and the cultivation of hops with them. In recent times Flemish missionaries have gone to and worked all over the world.

There is a theory that the Flemish had a hand in England's most popular summer sport. According to David Terry of the British Society of Sports History, "the Flemish probably moulded the traditional game of stoolball into something we recognise as cricket. However," he adds, guarding against the wrath of English gentlemen at so idolatrous a suggestion, "there is much we need to know about Flemish bat and ball games in the sixteenth century before we can reach a conclusion on their involvement in cricket."

Anyway Clement Attlee's statement that "the trouble with Europeans is that they don't play cricket" can't pass uncommented, if only because I was always under the impression that the English are Europeans too. But more of that in Chapter 6.

As a historical aside, one of the more distinctive names that crops up in East Anglia and other eastern counties is the surname 'Death': it sounds ominous to English people, but is probably explained by the fact that the family came from the French-speaking Belgian town of Ath *(de Ath)*. Edward III's wife was Philippa of Hainault, the province in which Ath is located. She was born in Valenciennes but, before she married Edward, spent years of her early life in Mons which is little more than 20 kilometres away.

The Spanish occupation of the Low Countries also prompted a lot of Flemish protestants to move northwards. Most of them abandoned Antwerp for the Randstad area of Holland, but others moved further north. For example Hamburg and Altona, the latter a town in its own right at the time, welcomed a small but influential community of Flemish Mennonites, many of them active in textiles and shipping.

The Flemish also ventured south. The Portuguese discovered the Azores in the second half of the 15th century but, by 1490, the couple of thousand Flemings who settled there had such an impact on the local culture that they were called 'the Flemish islands'.

The spirit of adventure had also been very much alive in Wallonia, from early on. In the mid-12th century, members of the Augustinian order settled in what was eventually to become the Polish city of Wrocław. They brought with them the Belgian art of brewing, for which Silesia subsequently became famous. Intriguingly, their district of the town was known to the locals as *platea gallica*, which indicates that the Walloons were identified as Gauls (Celts) rather than as Franks.

A substantial number of Walloon emigrés also settled in Hungary in the 12th century at the invitation of King Béla IV, and Walloon ironfounders helped develop the Hungarian iron and steel industry in the 19th century.

From one end of Miami Beach to the other

I offer the following story, recounted to me by a man on a train, as an example of Belgian opportunism and entrepreneurialism.

My informant imported beachwear, primarily for sale in Belgium. Due to strikes and stoppages, his Italian manufacturer was nine months late with that year's fashions. Our Belgian felt obligated to accept the product, despite the fact that the summer season was over, for the sake of good future relations with his supplier. But where could he sell some thousand items of beachwear in late-Autumn?

After due reflection, and although he had never seriously tackled the market before, he thought Miami might be worth a try, particularly since he knew someone in the trade there who, despite limited resources, had good local contacts. So our man took an Air Bahamas flight at less than half the scheduled rate and, with his friend, combed the waterfront shops from one end of Miami Beach to the other. He disposed of all his merchandise before he even got three-quarters of the way along, selling at half the average price for Belgium and accepting payment direct. He also persuaded his customers to guarantee reimbursement of a sum equivalent to the US import duty if this was waived retrospectively - which it was. So he cleared his stocks, covered his costs, eventually made a modest profit on the deal, and kept his supplier happy.

He also opened a new market!

The technology of Walloon smiths was transferred to Sweden's iron industry in the 17th century (the 'Walloon Process'), and Walloon glassmakers from Namur, Liège and Jumet contributed to Finland's first glassworks in Nötsjö at the end of the 19th century. A lot of Walloons also emigrated to Canada's Quebec province: they may have felt comfortable there because their French is rather similar in intonation and accent.

Over 200,000 Belgians are estimated to have emigrated to the United States between 1820 and 1975, many of them working in the iron and steel industries. Belgian engineers made a massive contribution to the rail networks of South America, Africa and China, not just laying the permanent way but supplying rolling stock, tunnelling machines, even stationary winding machines such as the one that used to operate the Langreo incline in the Spanish province of Asturias.

At the time of writing, it is estimated that over half-a-million Belgians are living and working abroad. Not bad for a country of just over ten million!

Erps and Kwerps

This 'get up and go' quality, so evident when Belgians find the need or opportunity to leave the country, is notably absent within the narrow confines of Belgium itself. I consider I now know the country far better than most of its citizens. Roots go so deep that nothing will persuade them to explore the land outside a modest radius of maybe 50 kilometres: on the rare occasions they feel obliged to go further, they race down the motorways, turning neither to left or to right.

I had spent something like thirty years thinking about writing a book about 'the cultures of Belgium'. Some of it was ready when I realised I had bitten off more than I could chew. I should have been aware of this much earlier on, when I had committed the cardinal sin of thinking an inhabitant of Lier was an Antwerpenaar.

In fact it was only much more recently, when researching for that never-to-be book, that I discovered not only that Herve on the eastern slopes of Wallonia had a different culture from nearby Verviers, but that there were two cultures in Verviers itself, depending on which side of the River Vesdre people lived. This is partly explained by the fact that, nearly three centuries ago – at a time when, incidentally, the country was temporarily a component of the Austrian Netherlands – the north side of the river was in the Duchy of Limburg while the south side was part of the Principality of Liège.

Another example is the 'twin' towns of Auvelais and Tamines, divided by the river Sambre and now known collectively as Sambreville. If only because of their different commercial destinies, they developed contrasting cultures: in the 19th century Auvelais was already a glassmaking town while Tamines was the site of three important coalmines. Yet even Tamines had two cultures: the upper half of the town was working class and owed its allegiance to the County of Namur while the lower half, closer to the river, was bourgeois and took its inspiration from the Principality of Liège. Belgians in fact are relatively un-class-conscious but, even so, birds of a feather do have a habit of sticking together.

The same kind of thing tends to happen in Flanders, and not just in Zonhoven. Take the TGV from Brussels to Lille and you cut right through the middle of the town of Halle, parallel to the old main line. Long before the arrival of the high-speed train, this town had two distinct cultures, depending on which side of the tracks people happened to live.

The coup de grâce to my never-to-be book on 'Belgium's cultures' came when I met a man from the Flemish village of Zaventem (which also happens to be the home of Brussels National Airport) and he told me he had married a girl from the area of Erps-Kwerps (I lie not!) some five kilometres away. He finds the two cultures so different that he goes back to his parent's home in Zaventem as often as he can.

I never did work out whether the issue was the difference between Zaventem and Erps-Kwerps or his relationships with his mother and his mother-in-law, but I decided that, after thirty years, it was time to give up. My determination was reinforced by the inadvertent comments of a native Erps-Kwerpsian who made me understand that there were even differences between the culture of Erps and the culture of Kwerps.

Since then, a Flemish friend has told me that the street he was born in was split down the middle, with the Catholics ranged on one side and the Socialists on the other. So fifty years ago, while class was of little importance, religion and politics still meant something to the Belgians.

Once again, as so often applies to things Belgian, the only appropriate way to describe the spirit of localism is as charming but surreal. One of the greatest ironies – among the many ironies in this blessed but benighted country – is that Flanders started out as a Duchy of the Kingdom of France where the elite and administrators spoke French, while the official language of the province of Brabant, within which nestles the now mainly French-speaking capital of Brussels, used to be Flemish! Read a history of that city in the 14*th* century and you will find that the notables had names like Wesemael, Duvenvoorde, Rotselaer, Withem and Meldert.

Maybe all this confusion helps explain why, when helping a consultancy company to classify European cultures in groups of countries, we not only couldn't decide where to put the French, which is hardly surprising, but also couldn't decide what to do with the Belgians, which came as more of a shock.

In fact you can't make much of Belgium today if you ignore the politics of the past. An object lesson for me was provided by my experiences in the German-speaking *Ostkantone* which I talked about in my first book, *We Europeans*. Annexed by the Kingdom of Belgium in 1918 and subject, before and after, to the historical irrationalities that are typical of this crazy part of the world, the area's inhabitants became more Belgian than the Belgians.

The key to their search for a revised identity - which runs completely counter to the attitudes of Belgians of longer standing, both Flemish and Walloons - is a nasty little episode at the end of WWII, when the government arbitrarily deprived those who had continued to work under the Nazi occupiers (as administrators, schoolteachers, etc) of their civil rights.

Was die Mentalität angeht, so stimmt es, dass wir Deutschsprachige keine Wallonen sind, sondern Eupener, Kelmiser, Büllinger, Manderfelder, usw...

(As for mentality, it's true that we German speakers aren't Walloons, but folks from Eupen, Kelmis, Büllingen, Manderfeld, etc...)

Comment on Internet blogsite serving the Ostkantone

So they're no different from any of the others, Walloons included!

This act of civic vindictiveness produced a generation, now emerged from college, that is distancing itself as much as it possibly can from the German culture. In the circumstances, the only way out is to be 'Belgian'. When Edward Mortimer of the *Financial Times* asked one of them what he would do in the event of the break-up of Belgium, he replied: "We are the only real Belgians... If Belgium breaks up, we'll probably ask to join Luxembourg." Strange comment on our times!

Equally strange is some of the recent history of the *Ostkantone*. There is a town tucked into the corner bordering Germany and the Netherlands which used to luxuriate under the name of 'Neutral Moresnet'. It, and its neighbouring community of Kelmis/La Calamine, were once home to a zinc carbonate or smithsonite mine, now abandoned. But the site was of sufficient strategic importance in 1815 to make it the subject of a condominium between the Kingdom of the United Netherlands and the Kingdom of Prussia. The former was supplanted in 1830 by the Kingdom of Belgium and the latter, in 1870, by the Deutsches Reich. But throughout, until the abandonment of the mine early in the last century, Moresnet remained admirably 'Neutral'.

With this kind of thing going on around them, it's hardly surprising that people in this part of the world also opted for localism. Like a French bedroom farce – with so many strangers popping in and out of their *Lebensraum* throughout history – the Belgians simply decided to hide under the sheets...

Of course there are other European hotbeds of localism, particularly Italy (there are fierce rivalries between 'city states' like Parma and Piacenza, Modena and Bologna) and, residually (most of all in the thinking), Germany. Regional pride and traditions are important in countries like France and Spain too but, precisely because these are larger and less densely populated areas, they do not evolve in the same way as the intense microcultures of tight little countries like Belgium, Ireland or the northern counties of the UK.

What Belgium is all about...

"Soft drinks were available but, even at 10:40 a.m., everybody preferred beer. Crushed plastic cups littered the ground on which stood two 30-something men, each sporting a racing jersey.

Since they declined to give their names – 'Why should we?' one asked reasonably – they may be labeled knowledgeable sources who spoke on the condition of anonymity.

'We're here to see Museeuw, of course,' the first source said. 'This is the last time he'll be in a Tour of Flanders. One more victory and the record is his alone. Also, we're here to see the race itself.'

'What he says goes for me,' the second source confirmed."

Excerpted from an article by Samuel Abt in the International Herald Tribune, April 6, 2004. Sadly, Museeuw didn't win...

6. What others know about Belgium and the Belgians...

"He is good natured and accommodating, and speaks the Belgium, German and English languages."

Algoma Record Herald, Wisconsin (USA), 19 August 1897

It will have been evident from the rather elaborate joke at the start of Chapter 2 that people have funny ideas about the Belgians. At least the Wisconsin journalist who summed up his perception of 'the average Belgian' in the words above kept it sweet and simple: Belgium does indeed have three official languages, but not the ones he lists. He also had a better excuse than a British professor who, in 1864, wrote of "the Walloons or inhabitants of Flanders" (how about that?). Yet sometimes I am inclined to think that, in their understanding of their neighbours, the British have retrograded in the last 150 years.

I have a quarrel with three groups of perpetrators in particular, the British, the Americans – and the French. The trouble with my fellow-Brits is that, not only are we all too often not *'of* Europe', we even seem to question whether we are *'in* Europe'. To me, when I look at a map it seems a geographic certainty: Europe is by far the nearest continent to the British Isles. Moreover, if we trouble to go back 10,000 years, we see that the British Isles were linked to the Continent by an umbilical land-cord.

Yet this doesn't prevent British TV weather people, when they have dealt with the drizzle at home, talking about "the weather in Europe." Nor does it prevent BA pilots – and I speak from personal experience – proudly announcing over the intercom that "we are now leaving Europe and the weather in Britain is fine."

Not long ago I heard of two British delegates to a professional conference in Waterloo, the site of the battlefield, who got no further then Waterloo Station in London. Evidently they hadn't heard of what British historians tell us was one of the greatest victories of all times, though not for the French. Maybe they thought the battle was fought in Lambeth. At least they reached the South Bank of the Thames in their search.

A propos, a recent study showed that one out of every ten British respondents thinks the Battle of Trafalgar was fought in London's Trafalgar Square (in the fountains presumably)!

The British love to think of themselves as a people apart, despite all the evidence to the contrary. For delusion at its looniest, go to the website of the British National Party and read the article 'The British – a mongrel race?' In strict contradiction to what the BNP thinks, far from having any racial distinction – and there we are like most of the peoples of western Europe, the Finns and the Basques excepted – we are a sublimely bastard folk. The Ancient Brit element has been submerged in successive waves of Celtic (central Europe), Anglo (Denmark), Saxon (Germany), Norman (Scandinavia/France), Danish and other genes. No connection with the Continent? Recent studies have even suggested that there are long-term genetic links with Spain...

One of the questions in an opinion poll conducted by the London Business School in 1998 among corporate chief executives was "how many European languages (including your own) do you speak fluently?" A number of British captains of industry said "none at all," suggesting not only that they were devoid of all language skills, but that they didn't even realise that English was a European language! This illustrates a state of mind that is dangerously subversive, whether it is unconscious or wilful.

Rue the day...

We travelled in a big truck through the nation of France on our way to Belgium, and every time we passed through a little town, we'd see these signs "Boulangerie," "Patisserie," and "Rue" this and "Rue" that, and rue the day you came here, young man. When we got to our hundred and eightieth French village, I screamed at the top of my lungs, "The joke is over! English, please!" I couldn't believe a whole country couldn't speak English. One-third of a nation, all right, but not a whole country.

From: Kenneth Tynan, 'Show People', talking about the American film director and actor, Mel Brooks, who eventually got to Belgium and found that a lot of English is spoken there.

Simple ignorance

At least, in the case of the Americans, it is not wilfulness but simple ignorance. There is a widespread tendency, reinforced by the lack of media interest, not to look outwards: according to the *National Geographic Survey* of 2004, only 23 out of 56 young Americans know the whereabouts of the Pacific Ocean!

But how many Europeans can position the 50 US mainland states on the map of America? So why should the Americans necessarily be better informed on the geography of Europe?

Yet the ignorance is at times excessive, particularly when it comes to Belgium. The Wisconsin journalist who penned the quote at the head of this chapter should have known better since there were – even in those days – a lot of people of Belgian descent in Wisconsin. But he can perhaps be forgiven, since he wrote this over a century ago. By comparison, I only recently stumbled across a US-based website that talks about "the island of Guernsey in Belgium."

One of the most authoritative American books on cultures, otherwise well researched and well reasoned, starts off the chapter on the Belgians with this disconcerting statement: "...the people of Belgium, both the Flemish (of Dutch ancestry) in the north and the Wallonians (of French ancestry) in the south..." Ancestry, my foot! Going into greater detail it talks of Limburg, where "German is the native language": that will come as a surprise to most

Limburgers. And taking a broader view, the same book claims that the mildness of the Belgian climate is "due to the Gulf Stream off the coast." The Gulf Stream may be guilty, but it's not exactly "off the coast."

I have met Americans, generally from the mid-West, who think Belgium is a state in Africa (echoes of the ex-Belgian Congo) and I have met many who, like a lot of Brits, think the only language spoken in this country is French. Come to think of it, most foreigners fail to realise that the country's majority population is Flemish and the majority language is Dutch.

I have even come across an American who was at least trying to work out for himself what the language spoken in Belgium might be. He used his powers of deduction: "The French speak French and the Dutch speak Dutch so, logically, the Belgians speak Belch."

One American, Eugene Hartley, got closer to the truth in 1946 when he researched American attitudes to 35 groups of foreigners. Three of these groups had bogus names invented by Hartley, but they were accepted without question by the participants as real. Indeed perceptions of these three groups turned out to be even more negative than those of the 32 genuine nationalities! And what were these three groups called? Danerians, Pyreneeans... and Wallonians!

Speaking of the latter, an American interculturalists' bible which tells you how to do business in sixty countries states, along with other dubious assertions, that "the Walloons feel

Marriage in Belgium
(à l'américain)

Belgium, a country with close traditional family ties, has a high Catholic population. According to Christian religious beliefs, women are expected to be virgin and their marriages are monogamous.

Although Belgium is a highly modern country with international businesses, cars are not used for dating as much as in most industrialised countries. Single people can still walk down cobblestone streets to cafés or shops where they can easily become acquainted with members of the opposite sex. Being picked up at one of these spots is normal and is not considered in bad taste. Otherwise, families and close friends introduce couples.

Huh?

From: Carolyn Mordecai, Weddings, Dating and Love Customs of Cultures Worldwide, (Nittany Publishers, Phoenix, AZ, 1999), winner of the 1999 ABPA Glyph Award of the Arizona Book Publishing Association.

that they are superior to the Flemish." Quite the opposite, the Flemish definitely know they are superior to the Walloons.

Perceptions can be strange even after people have arrived in a country, especially in the early days. I was dumbfounded when, counselling an American woman expatriate who had been in Belgium a couple of months, she complained bitterly about "all the spitting in the streets." I can hardly remember a single case in all the years I have been here. Maybe she was frequenting the bits of Brussels I rarely go to...

Southward parody, northward familiarity

Of all the three – Americans, British and French – it is the French who have the least excuse for being so cavalier with what are territorially, though not culturally, their closest neighbours. Experience has led me to the conclusion that, while the French may be a little more myopic than the British, their understanding of their neighbours is very selective: northwards they treat them with familiarity, southwards they parody them.

The French don't seem to know who their real friends are. In the 18th and 19th centuries, with the best intentions I like to think, they projected a strange and very subjective interpretation of the world to their south. Despite the efforts of Catherine de' Medici and other historical celebrities, the Italians were considered to be frivolous. Over the years the French did a great job of ridiculising the people south of the Alps, as Italian author Luigi Barzini has pointed out in a number of his books.

By comparison the Spanish – thanks in part to the artistic exertions of folk like Bizet, Merimée and others – were seen as gypsy-like, party-minded, untidy and exceedingly dirty.

This last point is an absolute travesty of reality because as a race, with the inevitable exceptions, the Spanish are meticulous in matters of personal hygiene.

While many of these perceptions still persist, the French at least had the authority of Blaise Pascal and the presence of the Pyrenees to excuse themselves: "Truth on this side of the Pyrenees is falsehood over there" *("Vérité au deçà des Pyrénées, erreur au delà")*.

Yet the geography north of 'the Hexagon' seems to pose as big a problem for the French as the Pyrenees. Perhaps the fact that France is intimately related geographically with Belgium – there is no natural frontier between the two countries other than the forests of the Ardennes to the east – encourages the French to conclude that the Belgians are close enough to be overlooked. I first had my attention drawn to French lack of knowledge of, or interest in, the Belgians by a reference in a French magazine to *'Audenaerde, un banlieu de Bruxelles'*. Oudenaarde is in reality separated from the Belgian capital by a good 60 kilometres of relatively open country.

The French don't even realise that so much of their presumed talent in the arts is, in fact, Belgian. As Pierre Rapsat, the late lamented Belgian singer who found fame and fortune in France, said with reason: "Belgium is poorly known and poorly understood" *("La Belgique est mal connue et mal comprise")*. Other Belgians who have flourished in the French entertainments industry include the TV presenter Christine Ockrent, the comedienne Annie Cordy and the singer Johnny Halliday, a.k.a. Jean-Philippe Smet.

To judge from reactions, the Belgians - Flemish and Walloons - seem to feel they have been dumped in much the same boat as the Italians and the Spanish. According to a recent study, Belgian businessfolk of both communities find the French arrogant, flowery of tongue, rich in false promises, often poorly prepared and, frankly and surprisingly, not that good at figures.

While the true character of the Belgians is obscured by familiarity and a smokescreen of bad (French) jokes, it is geography again that challenges the French perception of the Dutch: the culture is simply too far removed, both physically and intellectually. I once met a French university student who had no idea where the Netherlands featured on the map of Europe (he probably thought they were still under water). Equally significant and equally ill-informed geographically was the question put to me by a French student from Lille University who hitched a ride from me on his way to the Netherlands. "What," he asked, "is the skiing like in Holland?" I was too astonished to give a coherent reply.

Evidence of French misconceptions is available in a brochure published by nothing less than the French Ministry of Tourism, with the aim of encouraging French caterers and hoteliers to be more considerate towards foreign tourists visiting their beautiful country. It describes the Dutch in the following words: "The Dutch, a mixture of the British and German cultures, are the most representative of the Anglo-Saxons" *("Les Néerlandais, mélange de culture britannique et allemande, sont les plus représentatifs des Anglo-saxons")*.

Watch out for the wattman!

Another memorable lesson came many years later, when I was working in Brussels. I had parked in a less than ideal way. In fact, I had left my car on the tram tracks. While I sat blissfully ignorant in a pub, drinking beer with my Belgian colleagues, my car was making dozens of their compatriots late for dinner.

Of course, the tram driver could easily have pushed the car out of the way. The door was open and it was a small car. But in Belgium that's not how it works. Tram drivers don't push cars out of the way. On the contrary, tram drivers take great pleasure in scratching their heads as they contemplate their overtime and as their passengers fume. No, tram drivers don't push cars - tram drivers call the police who call tow trucks, leaving everybody in the tram to stew.

I had managed to block two trams for almost two hours in the middle of rush hour. The tram authority, I was told, would fine me $30 per minute per tram. And those were 1975 dollars.

All I could think to do was to throw myself on the mercy of the tram authority, so I wrote a letter apologizing profusely. I was sincerely sorry for the discomfort and inconvenience I'd caused the passengers.

I never mentioned the potential pain to my own wallet. I explained that I had only just arrived in Belgium (relatively speaking three years is just arriving) and that I didn't realize that parking on the tram tracks could cause such a problem. It was one of the best

*letters I have written in my long career as a copywriter.
I didn't expect it to work.*

*A very shrewd French lady, Jacqueline, our office
manager, offered to translate my letter into French.
She only changed one thing, my title. I had used the
lowliest title I could think of - something like Assistant
Account Co-ordinator - hoping the authorities would
take pity on a lowly working stiff.*

*Jacqueline promoted me to International Director.
She knew the Belgian mentality better than I did. I sent
the letter and I never heard another word about my
transgression. But I did learn a crucial lesson: knowing
who you're doing business with can have important
financial rewards.*

*As an American, I assumed a fellow human being
would take pity on a poor wretch. Jacqueline made no
such assumption. She knew that Belgians fear the rich
and powerful. They believe there are always wheels
within wheels and important people have mysterious
powers that can harm you if you cross them. Even if
you're right - especially if you're right.*

Richard Liss, an American expatriate in Brussels.

Apart from being calculated to upset the Dutch, the British
and probably the Germans too, this statement is – for
English eyes and ears – a gross distortion of the cultural and
ethnic realities. Yet the truth is that the French, perhaps
because they feel so different, have a broader interpretation
of what qualifies as 'Anglo-Saxon'. They go back to the

historical origins and include all the peoples that contributed to the strange and confused civilisation that ultimately became England. Curiously, they don't seem to include the Danes – yet, in today's geopolitical terms, the Angles came from Denmark.

Euroscopie, a seminal book on the European reality by an eminent French sociologist, speaks of the fact that "the Dutch seem to have no particular views on the Danes, despite the fact that they share a common frontier" *("Les Néerlandais semblent hésiter à se prononcer sur les Danois, bien qu'ayant une frontière commune avec eux")*. Whatever happened to a sizeable slice of north-western Germany? And some time ago Le Monde managed to place an English south coast town in the London suburbs: "Littlehampton, dans le banlieu de Londres" (French centrism seems to encourage them to include everything possible, including Oudenaarde, in the suburbs of big cities).

About the same time, seven out of 10 people in a French opinion poll located Amsterdam somewhere halfway between Copenhagen and Moscow...

Brussels, **Belgium** and Beyond

7. God bless Belgium!

"I will try to make your stay easier in this country which is very beautiful and contains more than one would dare to imagine."

Michel de Ghelderolde, quoted by Renée C. Fox
in her book *In the Belgian Château*

Most expatriates living here today agree that "Belgium is one of Europe's best-kept secrets." The beauty and variety of its landscapes are as little appreciated by the rest of the world as the character of its people.

After more than thirty years in this country, I have the conviction that the Belgians – all Communities and communities combined – are decent, honourable folk who deserve a better reputation than the one they currently earn from their fellow-Europeans.

Being human, they have their failings and their exceptions, including some notorious paedophiles: regrettably, you have to go a long way to find a country that has a clean record in this respect. As for the much talked-about trivia like bad driving and canine refuse, well, I find that Belgians drive no worse than other Europeans these days – though the Belgian authorities are still investing in major campaigns to cut the accident rate – and the risk of slipping on the Brussels sidewalk is minimal.

Belgium is an innately democratic country. It produces decent human beings at all levels of society - individuals whose only fault lies in the fact that other people know they are Belgians and therefore tend to make jokes about them because of their accents. The worst offenders are the French, yet what the French really understand about *égalité* would fit on the little finger of a Belgian's left hand. In the view of Michel Born, a sociology professor at Liège University, Belgian society is a much more progressive, diversified and multicultural democracy than anything France can pretend to.

This innate humanity even extends to the Belgian political classes who, god knows, have their critics – in the case of the inter-Community squabbles, with good reason. It's worth remembering that it was a Belgian government, not a French one, that insisted on a provision in the ill-fated European constitution that all EU policies must "take into account the guarantee of adequate social protection, the fight against social exclusion."

Unfortunately, 'the fight against exclusion' is not furthered by a troubling remnant of Belgium's political evolution: the pernicious carving-up of appointments to the judiciary and the diplomatic establishment in proportion to the weight of the political parties in the legislature.

For those coming from more formally structured societies, the methods of Belgian politicians may at times surprise, but as individuals they are approachable and real. It has been my lot to meet a number of them – Robert Urbain, Herman De Croo, Mark Eyskens, Guy Cudell, Jos Chabert, Marie Arena, Annemie Neyts, Robert Collignon, among others – and they have all impressed me by their accessibility and absence of flummery.

Herman De Croo figures prominently in Derk-Jan Eppink's efforts to explain the Belgian character in his book *Belgian Adventures*: "'The language barrier doesn't exist here', said De Croo cheerfully. He wanted nothing to do with Flemish nationalism, flag-flying and language disputes. 'It's only the provinces far from the linguistic border that get excited about language issues. Here we hardy notice it. People just get on with enjoying life.'"

De Croo lives in the East Flanders village of Michelbeke, seven kilometres north of the linguistic border. It's surprising how much difference a little distance can make. Take the old road due south from Brussels and, within seven kilometres of the centre you pass the old hillside suburb of Linkebeek, where the Community politics are poisonous. Drive on another four and you arrive in Alsemberg, where the staff at the local furniture supermarket treat you most courteously in any language you want. Of course, there's money involved...

One expatriate witness to Belgian commonsense is Bernard Tobin, who was Managing Director Europe & Middle East of Rolls-Royce/Bentley. In this capacity he invited an international group of automotive journalists to demonstrations at the Hungaroring circuit: there were

Brits, Germans, Italians, French and Belgians. They all behaved to type, except the Belgians. Far from being dumb and disorganised as the stereotype has it, they were in Bernard's words, "professional, respectful, helpful and friendly." The organising team, mainly British, preferred them to all the others - even to the British hacks, who spent most of their time drunk.

The poor public image of the Belgians is not helped by the fact that, with the world at large, they have a marked tendency to sell themselves short. The Flemish rank-and-file is confident enough in its inherited culture, reinforced by the exhortations of its politicians, but many Belgian French-speakers (awed by the pretensions of the French French, who want to feel cleverer) tend to be self-deprecatory, even at times making fun of themselves. Yet, as Englishman John Mole says in his book *Mind Your Manners*, "Walloons resent being regarded as quaint Frenchmen."

An Australian businessman I interviewed for my book *EuroManagers & Martians* summed up his understanding of the Belgians, Flemish and Walloons, in these rather condescending but revealing words: "They want to be good friends with everyone. They are comfortable with compromise, in fact they don't like black-and-white situations. Rather than make the big decisions, they would prefer somebody else played the boss."

Baldwin Klep, a Dutch executive search consultant who lives in Belgium and has a French-speaking Belgian wife, thinks this has a lot to do with history: "The Spanish occupation of the Low Countries almost destroyed Flanders. The elite emigrated northwards into the United Provinces – as a result half the population of Haarlem was Flemish for a time – and the ones who stayed were diminished by the experience. Ever since then, the Flemish psyche has been traumatised."

Subsequently the Flemish had to digest, in the 18th century, the emergence of the Brussels French-speaking bourgeoisie with their notions of *'standing'* (to use a quaint but totally unfounded anglicism) and, in the 19th century, the dominance of Walloon industry thanks to the coal and iron deposits in the southern half of the country. The Flemish felt intellectually, socially and economically impoverished. Later, with the swing of the economic pendulum, the Walloons began to feel the same way.

These experiences, largely fed by foreign influences and interventions, led to a social standoff between the two main communities in the country that, exploited feverishly by politicians, still rankles today.

Another consequence is that natural-born Belgians, whether they are Dutch or French speakers or something else, don't take anything for granted. They acquiesce in the fact that they are underestimated but then, says Klep, rise to the level of their own worth (often surprisingly high) and use the opportunity to take the initiative. The result is that they often excel in international business – both because of their unassertive manner and their natural intercultural affinities – and rate as some of the best potential around. "They are great change-makers and great team-builders," says Klep.

"They are very open, natural mediators and sensitive to other cultures." Despite their talent for self-effacement, they can be startlingly effective when they take on a top management role: many major international businesses, including Dutch ones, now have Belgians as their chief executives.

The Belgians have a disarmingly clever way of encouraging a false sense of security in others and then taking them by surprise. The best Belgian replique I know is the one that goes: "What's the quickest way to make a profit? Buy a Frenchman for what he's worth and sell him for what he thinks he's worth..." It's ironical that France itself takes its name from a Germanic tribe, the descendants of whom represent the majority in Flemish Belgium.

I suspect there is a lot of Frankish blood in Wallonia, as well as in the Flemish north. Belgian blood, like that of most other races, is extremely mixed – a reality that makes the recent decision of the Belgian Red Cross to establish separate blood banks for Flemings and Walloons rather ridiculous (maybe they will eventually establish a third for the German speakers of the *Ostkantone*).

The singer Pierre Rapsat made the often overlooked point that Belgium is in fact the product of a process of coming together. "I fully endorse this concept of a multifaceted Belgian nation." *("La Belgique est une nation de synthèse... J'appartiens totalement à ce concept de nation belge multiforme.")* Son of a Flemish father (with a French-sounding name!) and a Spanish mother, and singing in

French, he had – like a lot of other Belgians – his own example to prove his point.

No less than the Flemish Community Commission features a statement on its website describing the situation at the collapse of the Roman Empire in the 5th century [my translation]: "The Germanic Franks quickly constituted a majority in the north and a minority in the south of Belgium... It is indeed a linguistic frontier and not an ethnic one. So one should not imagine that the Flemish descend in a more or less direct line from the Germanic peoples or the Walloons from the Romans or the Celts. Neither the Flemish nor the Walloons are ethnically homogeneous, as far as anyone can trace their origins after so many centuries."

In fact, historians are still arguing over the possibility that the Walloons putative ancestors, the Belgae, had as much Germanic blood in them as they had Celtic...

How this very arbitrary but stable linguistic frontier developed, probably from the 5th century onward, is still a matter of conjecture. There is no physical explanation: no valleys, no rivers mark the line. One theory, now largely discredited, has it that it reflects the border between the ancient forests and more open marshy land to the north. Another is that it is the echo of another military frontier composed of forts and fortified villas running close to the Roman road linking Boulogne with Maastricht. The archaeologists are still looking for the evidence...

Whatever its origins, this linguistic frontier emphatically divides the country in two. Of course, as foreigners we tend to make fun of the Belgians' internecine quarrels. To us they seem to be out of place in a Europe that is coming closer together, even if some Belgians say that they are pointing the way ahead to a Europe where regions will share equal status with nation states. Not a bad idea, as it happens.

The same mental ghetto

At times the emphasis on drawing contemporary and often arbitrary linguistic lines across Belgian society strikes foreigners as vindictive or simply absurd, because of or despite the underlying reality of the language frontier.

Acutely conscious of the distinctiveness of their culture, and nervous about the implications of globalisation – an unease they share with the French and the Dutch, as evidenced by the recent referenda on a proposed European constitution – the Flemish electoral masses have allowed their concerns to mutate into xenophobia, fuelled by the agitations of right-wing extremists. Unfortunately, not only Arabs, Turks and Africans, but also the expatriate community generally... and inevitably French-speaking Belgians, tend to get caught up in the process, ending up in the same mental ghetto.

In more immediate and practical terms, the Flemish also feel they shouldn't have to go on dipping in their pockets to bail out the Walloons (the latter are making valiant efforts to revive the old spirit of entrepreneurialism, but the age of much of their manufacturing industry still holds them back).

But all of this is insufficient justification for Flemish initiatives like the annual mass pilgrimage around Brussels on foot and bike known as the *De Gordel* ('The Girdle'). The recipe for the event comprises love of nature and the virtues of physical exercise, unmistakably seasoned with a pinch of spiteful symbolism. As the promoters, the Flemish Sports Commission, say on their website, "Flanders will not abandon the Flemish edge [of Brussels]" *("Vlaanderen laat de Vlaamse rand niet los")*. OK, we know that.

Even more retrograde is the emergence of racism on the religious scene, as has happened in the otherwise delightful parish of Wezembeek-Oppem where the Flemish priest refused to celebrate mass for his French-speaking parishioners in their mother-tongue. Wanting to regionalise things like blood and the Belgian railway system is also going against the grain of history.

Another storm in the Community teacup was the tussle over the Flagey cultural centre (anything to do with culture is hypersensitive!), another step in the would-be *flamandisation* of Brussels – a clever strategy which has really left the French-speakers with their pants down. As a member of the rapidly growing immigrant population of the 'capital city' of Europe, this spat strikes me as vaguely comic. What is even more amusing – and evidence again of the surrealistic character of the country – is the fact that the two principal protagonists on the Flemish side are Bert Anciaux, the Flemish minister of culture, and Yves Leterme, the Flemish minister-president. An example of creeping francisisation?

Czech Mate

Our market research showed Czechs were not refined intellectuals at all... No! We discovered what they were: beer-drinking, working-class Catholics, rather like Belgians but less cultured.

Vladimir Zelezny of TV Nova talking to The Economist.

Of course, from the social history of the country in the last 200 years, it is easy to understand why the Flemish still tend to have a collective chip on their shoulders – though the phenomenon is less evident, I find today, in the younger educated generations. When, on top of it, you have Eurocrats and other Brussels residents outbidding locals for land and property in outlying communities like Overijse, you can understand the resentment. More often than not, these outbidders are foreigners – but the trend adds fuel to local resentment towards French-speakers even so. What was a bucolic Flemish Brabant village of grape-growers (the main square used to boast a large hand-painted sign with the memorable slogan 'Buy the Belgian grape: foodful and healing!') is now just another residential morass.

The inter-Community issue has recently been countered by a federal strategy for putting Belgium back on the international map and making its citizens a little prouder of their country. This strategy backfired on the law of international competence, but otherwise seems to have had some effect. The government's emphatic moral stance, fully supported by the electorate, at the time of the Iraq crisis

also did some good. It gave many Belgians the feeling
that they can, after all, be reasonably proud of themselves.
Rehabilitation, after a long time as moral outcasts, is
good for the soul.

Unfortunately, however, the Community syndrome still
distorts people's otherwise commonsense attitudes to life
and impinges on the country's relationships with the rest
of the world, fuelling the unduly dismissive views of many
foreigners who don't know Belgium any better. Geert
Bourgeois, the Flemish minister of tourism, had to deny
vigorously that he had instructed the Flanders tourist
office not to use the word 'Belgium' nor show the colours
of the national flag in its brochures for Germany.
But somebody did!

In attracting foreign investment, there is a cogent case for
'one-stop shopping', promoting the positive side of Belgium
through a federal agency: at least 'Belgium' is a label most
American businessmen can associate with, even if somewhat
inexactly, as the evidence in the previous chapter suggests.
Yet there is enormous resistance to the idea from both
intelligent people and some less intelligent ones, particularly
politicians – though there are signs that the different inward
investment agencies are now learning to work together.

The performance of Belgium's women tennis players – NB
one Flemish, one Walloon – in international championships
has done even more for people's self-esteem, even if the
federal government, in a typically Belgian example of
inspired opportunism, changed the taxation laws to

discourage Kim Clijsters from adopting Australian nationality. In place of the Flemish lion or the Walloon cock, some of her fans and those of Justine Hennin-Hardenne have been brandishing the Belgian national flag with, superimposed, the words 'the chocolate-makers'!

I think that history has now given the Flemish enough time to reassert themselves and, as intelligent people, they should learn to relax. There are indeed signs that the younger generation feels there are more important things to worry about: at best they find the inter-Community wrangle rather boring. Attitudes are tending to mellow: the principal issues these days are ones of substance and not merely motivated by political posturing.

The Walloons should relax, too. After all, both sides get on well enough together when no one is looking.

Individuals versus institutions

The combination of inter-Community politics and the surreal and occasionally seedy things that happen in this country have incited some very influential foreign media and other organisations to indulge in national character assassination.

The German magazine *Der Spiegel* did a vicious hatchet job some years ago when the Dutroux paedophile story surfaced. Even today, as well regarded an information source as *The Economist* newspaper group often adopts a superior and rather sneering tone when talking about events in Belgium. A recent *economist.com* newsletter gave the title 'Old balls' to a piece talking about the Atomium and then added insult to injury by announcing 'Another one' when referring to the arrest in Belgium of a paedophile who happened to be French and who had buried the body of his victim... in France. Maybe 'Another one' referred to the victim, but I think not.

There has been so much ill spoken of, or inferred about, the Belgian people by ignorant as well as supposedly well informed and well intentioned foreigners. Matters are not helped by the dismissive attitude of the country's neighbours, egged on by the French and Dutch and by a barrage of bad jokes about *fritten/frites*, 'Fons' and the rest. Even Brits tend to lose their reputed sense of fair play when talking about Belgium and the Belgians: there's a member of the British press corps in Brussels who talks regularly of 'Belgoslavia' (the Dutch pay a similar compliment when they refer to the almost-Belgian province of Limburg as 'Limbabwe'!).

Yet the blame, such as it is, lies essentially with Belgium's institutions and not with the people, other than the few that have occasioned these events. It is enough to glance at the *faits divers* columns of the French, German and British press to see that the same kind of thing goes on there as well, without becoming an international *cause célèbre*.

Because of their mix of caution and cultural ambiguity, Belgians have the unique and praiseworthy distinction of being people who are not in a position to take themselves too seriously, even if some of them are ridiculously serious-minded about their internal politics. Even if they don't underestimate their own worth, their self-esteem, when it shows, is relatively low-key. As Francis Heylighen explains, "Belgians may be one of the few nationals who will criticise their country, rather than make publicity for it, among people from other countries."

And yet a series of international surveys have pointed to Belgians' satisfaction with the quality of their lives. In 2003 the European Foundation for the Improvement of Living and Working Conditions conducted a survey involving 26,000 respondents in 28 countries (the 25 present member states plus Bulgaria, Romania and Turkey). This showed that, for satisfaction, Belgium came out in the top three on all aspects surveyed.

The judgement of those who really get to know the country and its people – including the many tens of thousands of 'privileged immigrants' now living in Belgium – is positive. Time and again, one comes across Americans, Brits and other Europeans who, after finding everything imaginable at fault with the country in their formative years here, have crossed that fatal five-year hump of residence in Belgium and find themselves stuck here, quite voluntarily, for the rest of their lives. They have acquired the art of being Belgian.

Ask them what it is that wins them over, and they will at best mumble something about 'quality of life'. Others might venture the thought that, the Belgians being essentially sensible and level-headed people who have learned historically to live with the vicissitudes of life, they show less stress symptoms these days than most other Europeans. They would be right!

Derk-Jan Eppink, the Dutch journalist, sums up the experience in the conclusion to his book *Belgian Adventures*: "After much reflection, I am now convinced that a Dutchman who comes to live in Belgium will never be the same Dutchman ever again. Belgium reforms you. Belgium deforms you – but in the nicest possible way." And, then, further on: "So what has Belgium changed in me? Above all, Belgium has helped me to put things in their proper perspective; to see that there is not just one universal truth, but a whole range of different truths; to understand that no one person is always right, but that lots of people are sometimes a little bit right." And that's a Dutchman speaking!

Other observers have difficulty in being as conclusive as this. A French journalist, Luc Rosenzweig of *Le Monde*, summed up many people's opinions of Belgium in a fairly minimalist way with these words: "There is no hidden vice nor exceptional quality in Belgium that could have escaped the attention of its neighbours or its masters. We should not expect this country to astonish us, either for the better or the worse. The Belgian brings humankind a gift worthy of his country: a modest gift but a congenial one." (*"Il n'y a en Belgique ni vice caché, ni qualité extraordinaire qui auraient échappé à la perspicacité de ses voisins ou de ses gouvernants. Il ne faut pas donc attendre de cette nation qu'elle nous étonne,*

*en bien ou en mal. Comme toujours, le Belge apportera a
l'humanité une contribution à la mesure de son pays: modeste,
mais sympathique.")*

Rosenzweig later became notorious for participating in a
Le Monde 'advertorial' scam and for saying that Brussels
reminded him of bombed-out Sarajevo. Despite the
depredations of the property developers he is referring to,
this is very much a 'live-and-let-live' country - an admirable
characteristic, even if it is prompted by the Belgian's
inclination to hunker down and avoid unnecessary exposure
to aggravation or anything else. It's all part of the art of
being Belgian...

The only criticism of Belgian society that I would
wholeheartedly endorse is the flagrant inadequacies of
the country's judicial system - in stark contrast to the
educational and public health systems which, at the
moment, are among the best in Europe: I say 'at the
moment' because government cost-cutting, in a
unsurprisingly pragmatic Belgian way, is threatening to
erode the infrastructure. Along with this country's historical
legacy of suspicion of authority, the current state of the
judiciary is sufficient reason to justify Belgians living
alongside, if not outside, the law. The fact that appointments
are politically arranged, as mentioned earlier, is sufficient
reason, for public scepticism.

The *Palais de Justice/Justitiepaleis*, the elephantine building
housing the capital city's law courts (NB: its architect did
not commit suicide after seeing what he had done), may

reasonably reflect the slowness with which Belgium's wheels of justice turn. In fact the law courts building in provincial Neufchateau, where some of the country's most seamy cases have been examined, is as impressive as a railway signal box. This fairly exemplifies the status of the country's legal system. Behind it lurks the reality of poorly paid officialdom: only 1 per cent of the government's budget goes to the legal institutions. Compare that with the national fortune frittered away in one way or another on the country's inter-Community affairs!

I hope a reinvigorated legal system, if it comes, will still not expunge the Belgian talent for interpreting the rules pragmatically according to the circumstances. A good example of this is a company I know that, owned and run by foreigners, got into financial difficulties through no fault of the owners. Lacking the means to resolve the problem in the short term, and not wishing to liquidate the business and penalise the company's creditors, they explained their predicament to a friendly Belgian tax inspector. He, in his personal capacity and at his own professional risk, worked through his network of colleagues to 'call off the dogs' and the company survived.

Imagine that kind of realism, entrepreneurialism and fellow-feeling from a British or a German tax inspector!

Belgians owe this pragmatism to living so long with the overweening international ambitions of their more powerful or bloodthirsty neighbours: the French, the Spanish, the Austrians, the Germans and, latterly, the Dutch. Over time, the Land of Cockaigne became the Cockpit of Europe. And the Belgians – Flemish, Walloons and others – found their own amiable ways of dealing with these realities.

They are now involved in the difficult process of learning to live together in a changing world. And yet their greatest and often unrecognised strength is that they have the best of both western European worlds, the Germanic and the Latin. They relate to, and take on board, the best qualities of both. The German and French Swiss have the same potential, but they are divided by the *Röstigraben*.

The Belgians, prepared to acknowledge it or not, have a facility for crossing this imposing cultural frontier precisely because it is an integral part of their history. That's part of the art of being Belgian. Rather than cutting themselves off they have, in their unassuming way, mixed in with a will.

Maybe the *economist.com* should, after all, be allowed the last word. After evoking the inter-Community tensions for those who still aren't aware of them, the May 2005 issue of the Cities Guide for Brussels said:

"More likely, however, the Belgians will stick together. For all the grumbling and animosity between the two main language groups, Brussels is a fundamentally peaceful and prosperous place."

If Wallonia manages to dig itself out of the hole it is in at the moment – with or without the help of the Flemish – all Belgium will be an example to the rest of Europe. Brussels, after all, is only a small part of Belgium and, in many respects, totally untypical of this small and surprising country.

Writing about the Dardenne brothers' success at the 2005 Cannes film festival, Leen Demaré, a Flemish mother-tongue columnist with the Brussels magazine *Zone 02*, said: "I was lucky enough to interview the two brothers. They started by apologising profusely for the fact that they didn't speak any Dutch, but they still greeted me with a friendly *'goeiendag'*. It doesn't bother me a bit that two heroes don't master the Dutch language and, as a result, I have to bring out my best French… We are in a 2 (3)-language country where we live within a stone's throw of another language community. We should be proud of being able to speak at least two languages… So, Luc and Jean-Pierre, your apologies are naturally accepted, *mais je vous remercie d'avoir gagné cette deuxième Palme d'Or pour notre pays. Merci.*"

Now, that's the spirit!

Brussels, Belgium and **Beyond**

8. Neighbours - the Dutch

"Crossing the Dutch frontier marks a difference not only in the character of the people but in the appearance of the landscape."

Patricia Carson, The Fair Face of Flanders

Compared with the Belgians, the Dutch are too dogmatic.

I wonder if my Dutch friends, who laughed all those years ago at my decision to live in Belgium, would react the same way now. The social angst is bigger in the Netherlands these days than it is in Belgium, while the quality of life is not all that much better than it was in the late-'60s. Those of the Dutch who can afford it are voting with their feet – either by settling in the Flemish Kempen region northeast of Antwerp (7,200 of them last year alone) or by emigrating further south.

There is even a website dedicated to the change in the two countries' relative fortunes: www.belgendoenhetbeter.nl ('Belgians do it better').

Belgian cartoonist Jean-Paul Picha is right when he says the best way to define a culture is by a process of exclusion, by differentiating it from the cultures of its neighbours. Belgium is a country that's difficult to define – but you know very well what it's all about when you leave the country.
And as Patricia Carson says and many eminent sociologists will confirm, the differences between the cultures of the Netherlands and Belgium, despite their geographic proximity, are enormous.

Perhaps the thing you notice most of all is the 'hermetic' nature of the cultures next to Belgium. France, to the south, owes its almost autistic character - see Chapter 9 - to the sheer size of the 'Hexagon' itself and the power of its cultures (*pace* the Bretons, the Basques and the people of the Pays d'Oc). Luxembourg is a cosy little bourgeois community all on its own. Germany owes its hermeticity to its inhibitions, creating what I call the Social Consensus Effect (SCE).
And the Netherlands is another 'closed' culture because of its degree of social organisation: the Dutch have such a finely tuned society that they automatically assume that everything works, when in fact it doesn't.

By comparison, Belgium is an open society. Sure enough, you dig down a bit and you find lots of hidden barriers – the spirit of localism again – but they are surmountable.

When you drive northwards into the Netherlands from Belgium, you enter a different world. The motorways narrow from four lanes to three, then two, and the overhead lighting disappears. Even the weather is different: cross the Rhine and the mist-and-drizzle-laden continental clime of Belgium gives way to a gusty-and-open-skies North Sea environment.

You realise you have passed in minutes from a gentle and expansive country into an essentially breezy and frugal one, the Netherlands. If you happen to cross the frontier on a country road you have the same effect in microcosm: the road gets narrower (and prettier due to the charming Dutch habit of using red herringbone-pattern road tiles in towns, rather than asphalt) and the houses get smaller.

Many people will tell you it is unrealistic to make comparisons between the Belgians and the Dutch: they are as unalike as chalk and cheese, the Dutch being the cheese of course. Geert Hofstede, the Dutch social psychologist and interculturalist, said that he had "found no other case in the world of two neighbouring countries having so much in common and still showing such differences in their mental programming;"

I would exclude the Dutch living south of the Rhine from this judgement: they bear some attitudinal and behavioural similarities to their Flemish neighbours of Belgian Limburg. There's even a very naughty Dutch joke that acknowledges the fact: "Q: What would be the effect on the national IQ of the Netherlands and Belgium if the Dutch province of Limburg was transferred to Belgium. A: The IQ of both countries would go up." No need to tell you how the Belgians respond to that…

The incompatibility of the two cultures was evident in 1816 when, in a brief and unproductive liaison, the two Low Countries – the United Provinces of the Netherlands and the *Pays-Bas* of Belgium – cohabited under a single king, William I, with twin administrative capitals in The Hague and Brussels. In his *Histoire de Bruxelles* Georges-Henri Dumont records that "according to most of the ambassadors here, the difference in temperament made it impossible to integrate the two populations." Yet in 2003, according to the Dutch Emigration Office, "Flemish affability" was instrumental in persuading many Dutch nationals to settle in Flanders.

The Belgian poet Georges Mogin ('Norge') said that his protestant ancestors emigrated from France to the Dutch Netherlands because of the Edict of Nantes. But, two generations later, the family moved southwards into what is now Belgium. They found the Dutch abrasive and the Belgians much more 'open' (so much for the closed shutters stereotype!). Even today, a Dutchman from the Randstad – the heart of Holland between Amsterdam, Den Haag, Rotterdam and Utrecht – stands out in any part of Belgium, north or south, like a sore thumb.

Edward Sikkens, a Dutch advertising executive who has spent many years in Belgium, says: "In my home country, Holland, we say 'all is possible, but we can't do anything about it' whereas, here in Belgium, they say 'it's all impossible, but we can work something out'."

Cultures express themselves at so many levels of life: basic value systems at one end of the scale – and here as much unites the Belgians, Flemish and Walloons, as divides the Flemish from the Dutch – and the trivia of life at the other.

The contrast between the Flemish and Dutch realities is more striking than that of any other pair of neighbouring European countries, even Germany and France. It is the outward expression of fundamental cultural differences which can only be explained in terms of environment and history. Much of the most populous part of the Netherlands faces out towards the North Sea. It is directly exposed to the elements, wind and water, and its people have devoted much of their energies to fighting or harnessing them.

The history of this part of Europe also features two different politico-religious destinies. When, in the second half of the 16th century, the Catholic Spanish occupied what were then the Southern Netherlands (today's Belgium), a good 100,000 members of the country's intelligentsia fled to the North (today's Netherlands). It took a long time for Flanders to recover from this intellectual and entrepreneurial impoverishment, while the Netherlands benefited immensely.

At least the two countries share a common language, common up to a point. Apart from some deviations in spelling, and vast variations in dialect, the way they actually express themselves differs distinctively. The mainstream 'Randstad' Dutch speak from the front of the mouth, the sounds tending to be sibilant as if their teeth were getting in the way: appropriate in a people who have coped historically with a windy and watery environment.

I have heard Dutch citizens express envy at the softer version of their language practised by the Belgians. Flemish Dutch is indeed more melodious, although some of its practitioners manage to make it sound like the relentless chatter of a machine-gun. Flemish women, in particular, will often acknowledge the comments of a companion with a mechanical 'ja, ja, ja, ja, ja' intended to signal agreement.

One of the problems with trying to compare two cultures is that the subject-matter itself tends to colour the analytical process. This is not a comment on my powers of assimilation: I speak Dutch no better than most Englishmen and my knowledge of the two cultures is based more on observation than detailed study. It is rather a tribute to the power of individual cultures to cast their spell on the observer and influence the manner in which he or she thinks about them.

The result is that I find myself discussing the Dutch culture in essentially formalistic and structural terms, whereas my approach to the Flemish culture is empathetic. This of course may have something also to do with the fact that, living in Belgium, my relationship with the Flemish culture is more intimate.

Dogmatic and pragmatic

Inevitably there are points of contact between the cultures. The two Limburgs, as the joke suggests, share a common sense of the romanesque. And every country contains elements that display a marked deviation from the norm. We English, like most other foreigners, tend to think of 'the Dutch' in terms of the Randstad people. We have no comparable point of reference when thinking of the Flemish unless it's Antwerp, Gent or Brugge, and then we are talking about different things! And that, the spirit of localism, is one of the charms of Flemish Belgium. The Netherlands also has its civic loyalties, but they are of a more formalistic and less visceral nature.

Dutch society is so emphatically well structured and organised, with its *zuilen* (the 'pillars' that represent the various denominational and other groups), its self-assurance, its democratic impulses and its tendency to moralise. Nothing at all wrong with any of this, except that you are constantly reminded of it. A group of my colleagues, German and Spanish, were discussing the Dutch art of conversation. "They simply don't dialogue," said one of them. "They just make statements..."

This also happens on Dutch television, where one of the cults ran a commercial with the following invitation, in Dutch of course: "If you want to know more about GOD, telephone .... (with number)"! Turn GOD around and you have the first three letters of DOGmatic, which is certainly a word that we English have been known to use to describe the Dutch. The word that first springs to mind to describe the Flemish - or the Belgians, come to that - is PRAGmatic. Neither of these words, 'dogmatic' and 'pragmatic', has a pejorative sense in my vocabulary. They are simply different forms of *Weltanschauung*.

The Dutch, in their mercantile period, had the opportunity to build a carefully structured and at times censorious society. Simon Schama offers an insight in his book *The Embarrassment of Riches*, where he talks about the classic Dutch counterpoint between materialism and morality: "We end, then, where we began: in the moral geography of the Dutch mind, adrift between the fear of the deluge and the hope of moral salvage, in the tidal ebb and flow between worldliness and homeliness, between the gratification of appetite and its denial, between the conditional consecration of wealth and perdition in its surfeit".

In fact the Netherlands is such a well organised country socially – and Dutch citizens so well trained civically – that this in itself can cause problems. People tend to ignore the more evident signs of need – for example youngsters sleeping rough in cardboard boxes under railway arches – because they are convinced there is an organisation, funded from their personal taxes, that will promptly take the matter in hand.

The mother-knows-best (or 'Dutch uncle') mentality of society also leads to a situation where, in the opinion of a Dutch business school professor, its citizens are so fine-tuned for life within their own society that they are ill-prepared for anything else. An eminent Swedish executive search consultant tells me that he has so far never found a suitable Dutch candidate for any of his international assignments.

One of the problems is conviction of one's own rightness. A belgicised Dutchman, Derk-Jan Eppink, understands the differences very well: "For a Netherlander 'openness' is saying what you think, irrespective of the consequences. For Belgians, 'openness' is saying what you think somebody wants you to say, with a very clear eye on the possible consequences." Yet, at the end of the day, as the British say, you can be Dutch and 'open' and still have a pretty closed mind, whereas Belgians may seem to be 'closed' but will still be receptive and sympathetic. That applies to both sides of this country - and that's the real difference between the Belgians and the Dutch!

By comparison with the well organised world of the Dutch, the Flemish culture reflects the ever-changing nature of an environment that was marked by a succession of generally uninvited intruders. This has inevitably produced a pragmatic, even opportunistic, attitude of 'let's make the best of it' and a real appreciation of the good things of life. Flemish attitudes – either a dour commitment to living well or a 'burgundian' or even rabelaisian enjoyment of such worldly pleasures – demonstrate an absence of inhibition rarely found in the Dutch. Bernard Tobin, the ex-Managing Director of Rolls-Royce/Bentley, says his company sold seven times more of its exuberant cars in Belgium than in the Netherlands.

Where the Dutch have evolved a supremely well structured and organised society, the Flemish are suspicious of authority (with reason) and often prefer to rely on their own wits and industry, supported by loyalty to their immediate circle. In the words of Dutch social psychologist Geert Hofstede: "There is more mutual trust between police and citizens in the Netherlands than in Belgium. Therefore in our country the police can rely more upon the help of the citizens in a crisis situation, and the citizens upon the police, than in Belgium."

In her book *The Fair Face of Flanders*, Patricia Carson makes the same point: "To the Dutchman, the Fleming is showy, wasteful and irresponsible. To the Fleming, the Dutchman is pompous, too well organised and, above all, too obedient to the state. To many Dutchmen the state is a friend, to the Fleming, if not an enemy; it is at least something to be avoided as much as possible."

This typically Belgian attitude, common also to Walloons, emerges moreover in a degree of passivity when dealing with authority, even at the humble and everyday level of the queue in the local post office. Bureaucracy, not just a monopoly of the Dutch culture, is accepted by Belgians with fatalism – but, compared with the Dutch, they are anarchists.

Suspicion of authority helps reinforce a remarkable feature of Belgian society that can perhaps be described as localism in microcosm: the continuing sense of family, something that died out in most of Britain decades ago. When the external environment is hostile, you retire into one of your own making.

Maybe that explains another difference when you cross the border after dark: the shutters on the Flemish side are down, but you can see straight into the living rooms of the Dutch. Visible evidence of their dedication to democracy and transparency?

Benewhat?

One of the most bizarre concepts favoured by international business – and there are some other bizarre concepts like lumping Europe, the Middle East and Africa together in something called 'EMEA' – is the idea of a 'Benelux' subsidiary.

Nothing could be more disruptive than to put the Dutch and the Belgians in the same barrel. This idea finds its origins in a politico-commercial arrangement, not a cultural reality (the idea of a customs union between France, Italy and Luxembourg might have stood a better chance of success, but for the fact that it would have been called 'Fritalux').

Speaking of food brings us to the most dramatic difference of all: Dutch frugality versus Belgian 'burgundianism'. The HR director of the Belgian subsidiary of a big Dutch company complained to me bitterly that, every time he was summoned to a day-long meeting at head office, the conference room door would open on the dot of midday and a big-footed woman would come in with a glass of milk and a cheese sandwich for everyone (the company was in the dairy products business). Yet, as he put it, "whenever they come to Belgium, they expect to be taken out to the best restaurant."

A Belgium-based regional headquarters is an outright provocation to the Dutch, while a Netherlands-based HQ will find its efforts sabotaged by the Belgians. So, whatever the solution chosen, the 'Benelux' management will have its time cut out. Any management decision will be openly challenged by the Dutch (they will want to know why, and won't give up until they're satisfied), whereas the Belgians will appear to acquiesce. Only weeks later will the management realise their new strategy has simply not been taken on board. It's not that Belgians are uncooperative – from many years experience I can vouch for the fact that they are wonderful team workers, industrious and loyal – it's just that something in their bones (foreigners, history, etc) tells them that it's better to hunker down and say nothing at the time...

In his book *Belgian Adventures*, Derk-Jan Eppink confirms the dilemma this poses for so-called Benelux managers: "A Fleming will not easily show when he is unhappy with something. Instead he will keep quiet and let you find out for yourself what the problem is. A Dutchman will always demand a forum in which to air his grievances. A Fleming will withdraw into his shell and pull up his defences [the 'bunker complex']. He will not openly complain but will express his displeasure by a policy of delay and non-cooperation. Nothing gets done and, before you know it, everything has ground to a halt. If you have a problem with a Hollander, it will quickly become visible. If a problem with a Fleming becomes visible, it is already too late."

A lot of intelligent and experienced Benelux managers have confirmed these behavioural differences to me. The exception that proves the rule as far as the Belgians are concerned is the experience of a British officer during the First World War (recounted by Francis Heylighen) who noted that his Belgian foot soldiers would ask why they were being ordered to do something and wouldn't do it until they got an acceptable reason from him. But this, in the Flanders trenches, was by definition a matter of life and death. At times like that, survival triumphs over cultural instinct...

Eppink has more to say about the differences. In Belgium, he says, "there is much more humour and an easier acceptance of life's ups and downs. By the same token, there is much less system and almost no planning... This is not necessarily a bad thing. A Dutchman will make a plan for everything and will then regard this plan as sacred. Anyone who is not willing or able to conform to the plan is instantly labelled as a troublemaker and excluded. The Flemish are much more flexible and can adapt quickly to changing situations. For a Dutchman, an agreement is inviolable, something written in stone [NB: but beware of the small print in a

Dutch contract!]. For a Fleming, an agreement is merely a temporary arrangement. If the circumstances change, the agreement can also be changed."

So, while the Belgians adapt to the circumstances, the circumstances have to adapt to the Dutch. Take the experience of a rank outsider, the Scottish chief engineer of one of the world's automotive giants, who discovered the difference for himself when he commissioned a Flemish Belgian civil engineering consultancy to supervise construction of a plant extension for a new production line. The consultancy hired a team of technicians specifically for the project. Some of them were Flemish, some Dutch.

A few weeks into the construction phase, up to which point everything had been running smoothly, our Scottish friend learned that the specifications for the new car model would require an additional finishing stage and that this would require x square meters of additional space. He called in the Flemish project manager and agreed with him on the changes: an end-wall moved y meters further out and six pillars repositioned.

The project manager, being Flemish and culturally attuned to change and compromise, had no problem with this. Nor did his Flemish engineers, who cheerfully did what they were told and never asked questions. But the Dutch engineers, when they heard of the changes, first wanted to know why and agonised over the situation, then had the greatest difficulty in refocusing their mental sights on the new objective (once they did, they worked as well as the Flemish).

The project was completed satisfactorily and on schedule, though not on budget. The Scottish chief engineer then called the Flemish project manager into his office and said: "We're certainly going to have another job like this before long and we'll certainly consider your company for the project. But it's on one condition: no Dutchmen on the team...!"

These differences underscore the essential incompatibility between the Flemish and the Dutch, even if they can be good friends – as, at the level of individuals, they often are. In her book Patricia Carson poses a rhetorical question: "Why not become part of the Kingdom of the Netherlands? Such an opinion, expressed in all innocence, is likely to provoke derisive comment. Very few Flemings want to become citizens of the Netherlands. They prefer to form the majority in a federal state, rather than to occupy a small corner of the Dutch kingdom, which would look upon them also with limited enthusiasm."

The feeling is mutual – and, when put to it, even the Flemish can warm to the idea of coexisting with the Walloons and the German-speakers in a federal state called Belgium!

9. Neighbours – the French

*"I wanted to capture the differences between Belgium and France,
differences that are more than just about language – even the
houses aren't the same."*

Belgian cinéaste Yolande Moreau talking to
the *International Herald Tribune* about her films.

Compared with the Belgians,
the French are too theoretical.

Travel south from Brussels and, just beyond the border,
you will find yourself traversing a wasteland of scrubby
hedgerows and bits of abandoned corrugated iron that
shrieks 'France'. You are witnessing the combined effects of
the centralism of French life and the 'laissez-faire' attitude
of many of its inhabitants.

The well-earned qualities of the French – intelligence, charm,
esprit – are not that evident when you approach the country
and the culture from the Belgian end. The bad jokes told by
the French get in the way and, to the lasting chagrin of the
Flemish, the northwestern corner of the country including
the splendid city of Lille (Rijsel!) was taken away from them
in 1713.

But these very positive French characteristics are sustained –
particularly in the most intelligent, charming and spiritual
members of the French establishment – by a voluntary
confinement to the 'hothouse' of French culture and what
I would venture to call *francisité*. French high society
is very hermetic.

Some people would go further. Rudolf von Thadden, a
German government adviser on foreign policy, says "the
French are an autistic nation." Autism, according to my
dictionary, is "absorption in imaginative activity directed by
the thinker's wishes, with loss of contact with reality". It is
associated with repetitive and compulsive behaviour, undue
focus on limited interests, and tends to impair relationships.
Well, yes.

In her book *Europeans* Jane Kramer, European correspondent
of *The New Yorker*, suggests the condition is linked to the
French collective subconscious: "History... has a pedagogic
function. It is only as 'true' as its usefulness in maintaining
proper attitudes toward being French – including the fierce
and oblivious identification Frenchmen have with France
and with everything they mean by France. Strangers tend
to see that identification as nationalism or chauvinism, but
it is much more primitive. A Frenchman identifies with
France the same way he lifts his chin and sticks out his
lower lip when he is puzzled – as a kind of reflex action."

There are a lot of ordinary French people (NB: French people
are rarely 'ordinary') who behave in a perfectly normal and

rational way. But, as a nation, they often give us foreigners the feeling that they are at least a little bit autistic.

The epithet applies most readily to the upper strata of French life, in particular the 'mandarin' class of graduates of the *Grandes Ecoles* – and notably the *énarques* of the Ecole Nationale d'Administration who claim most of the top posts in government and business. One of their number admitted in late-2002 to *The Economist* that "*énarques* are pretty smart individually, and pretty dumb collectively." From which the newspaper concluded that "the reason that they can be 'collectively dumb' is that they all come from the same educational mould, which makes their responses somewhat predictable." As a nation, the responses of the French are predictable as well.

Enarques are renowned for their *esprit de corps*, they stick firmly together even when one of them gets into trouble. I once asked one of their members what happens when an *énarque* makes a mistake. "An *énarque* never makes a mistake," he replied. I should have known better...

French politicians, too, have a tendency to respond in kind: 'messianistic' is not too strong a word to describe the presumptions of Charles de Gaulle (legitimately) and François Mitterand (illegitimately). Others, such as Giscard d'Estaing, have managed to create much the same impression through their mandarin-like mode of utterance. More recently, Jacques Chirac demonstrated similar self-absorption and *délusions de grandeur* when he reprimanded

Tony Blair with the words "I have never been spoken to like this before!" Not a moment too soon, as it happens. In short, to quote Philippe Méchet, a French opinion pollster: "We're a very royalist country, and we killed the king. So now we've monarchised the republic."

*Plus ça change, plus ça reste la meme chose...*The French presidency, living up on Nuage Neuf, is as removed from the French masses as Louis XIV was. But the problem is not just one of distance, it is a wilful divorce from reality. Hence the failed referendum on the European constitution.

René Descartes evidently never realised what he was letting the French in for. The Cartesian virus was potent and tenacious, spreading to all levels of thinking French society (the Frenchman-in-the-street, by contrast, is infected with a much more basic appreciation of what matters in life, namely himself to the exclusion of others). Richard Bernstein, the author of *Fragile Glory*, said in a post-referendum column in the *International Herald Tribune* that "French thinkers have been caught many times in the past having ideas more or less independent of any empirical basis – preferring lofty Cartesian speculation to fact-finding, or expecting reality to conform to concept rather than the other way around." Gallic deductive thinking, as opposed to the inductive approach of the Belgians and the Anglo-Saxons, puts concept before commonsense.

Autistic or not, the French are often excessively self-absorbed. Part of the problem is the difficulty of dissociating oneself as an individual from the concept of the nation: the

Frenchman (but not always the Frenchwoman) is brought up to view himself as a personification of his country's history and culture, whether that culture happens to be of the BCBG *(bon chic bon genre)* kind or of the *steack-et-frites* variety.

One cause of French autism is inevitably the weight of history, another is the sheer size, variety and beauty of 'the Hexagon' as the French choose to call their country. They have little reason to holiday abroad and, in the words of Catherine Wihtol de Wenden, a director of the French Centre for International Research (CERI): "There is always the idea that if you go elsewhere, it is because you are running away from a problem, that you have an adventurous side and that you are not really serious." The net result of all this is that France has the most hermetic society of any western European country.

Thanks to this hermeticism - and the inevitable historical mythmaking that is characteristic of all European nations, west and east - the French have been out of touch with much of the rest of the world for a very long time. They tend to sneer high-mindedly at the Belgians, their little northern neighbours with the funny accents. Belgian filmmaker Yolande Moreau's experience is typical: "We used to be looked on as clods and Belgian cinema was snubbed, but since the Dardenne brothers, we've come up in the world." Ultimately justice is done. In the meantime, the Belgians have to suffer a series of silly jokes which they retrofit and return with interest. The smokescreen this process creates may help explain French confusion over European geography to the north of the Hexagon.

The Pyrenees have historically obscured a proper appreciation of the Spanish. But the French also fail to realise that they owe an enormous amount to the Italians, who invented much of what is now considered to be the 'flowering' of French culture. When Catherine de' Medici moved to Paris to marry Henry II of France, she brought a number of things with her that have since proved of inestimable value to the French. The first was good cooking. Up to that time, French so-called cuisine was little better than the things that the English were eating (the French have raised their standards since then): large joints of vitiated meat, stews and the like.

The second thing that Catherine gave the French was perfume. Up to that time, the French smelled as bad as everyone else, so Italian perfumes helped them clean up their act. The result was two-fold: the emergence of the French perfume industry that dominates the world today, and a greater tolerance of the French for body odour, their own and that of others.

Napoleon, returning from a successful campaign in Egypt, sent an aide-de-camp on ahead to Josephine with the message: *"Ne te laves pas, j'arrive!"* The French had evidently acquired some rudiments of personal hygiene, even if they still believe today that something very organic called *le terrain* is vital to human health.

In reality their tolerance to body odour has limits. In 2002 the mayor of La Grande Motte beach resort near Montpellier felt constrained to issue free T-shirts to UK tourists. "Those

British," he said, "they come off the beach covered in sweat and suntan oil and they stink. It's enough to make other people – including me – feel sick."

At least it can be conceded that the French passed their perfumes – part of their adopted culture – onto the Swedes. In 1818 Sweden initiated what could be considered the first executive search assignment. The country needed a king to succeed the heirless Charles III and found an acceptable candidate in a pensioned-off Napoleonic marshal, Count Jean Bernadotte. The new monarch arrived in Stockholm with a bathtub (claimed to have been the first seen in that country) and a generous supply of Eau de Cologne. When granting audience, Bernadotte had his subjects sprinkled liberally with the imported product before saying *"approchez, Messieurs."*

But back to Catherine de' Médici. The third thing she brought with her from Florence was the habit of gesticulating – up to that time waving your hands and arms around was considered bad taste at the French court. This was perhaps the least praiseworthy of her importations...

The art of changing one's mind

Being supreme pragmatists, the Belgians are capable of changing their minds time and again – assuming that they make them up in the first place (and, if they do, they very probably keep their opinion to themselves).

By contrast, the French revel in giving and airing an opinion, maybe more than one at a time. But one of the things that became evident to me in the course of researching for my second book, *EuroManagers & Martians*, was that, where the typical German thinks changing one's mind on something important is a bad thing, the educated French person thinks it's a virtue. It's a sign that he or she has a lively and productive brain.

It is also a symptom of the scepticism of the French cartesian mind – a condition that I suspect may indeed precede Descartes, and which can deteriorate at time into mild suspicion or downright mistrust. It reflects a continual questioning or, as some foreigners would prefer to say, insecurity. An American wag suggested that, if Shakespeare had been French, he would have had Hamlet say: "To be or not to be, that is the question... but the question is badly formulated."

The readiness of the French to have second thoughts is the source of much aggravation for foreigners dealing with them in business. It is best, if somewhat extravagantly summed up in the words of a British management consultant, John McBride, whom I interviewed for my book: "You agree the points of principle with the French in the morning, then go off precisely on the stroke of one o'clock for a five-course lunch where you talk about everything except business. You go back home thinking everything's fine, only to receive a fax the following morning saying they disagree with at least one of the points of principle. I sometimes wonder whether the French only really think when they're digesting or asleep. This has happened to me at least a dozen times."

At least the five-course lunch is enjoyable, but he would have got just as good and far more productive a lunch if he had gone to Belgium instead.

"The French, the Italians and the Spaniards have a tendency to intellectualise and theorise everything," says an Italian investment banker. "A decision is a good one only if it has been changed seven times." Make that fourteen times for the French! This mind-changing phenomenon is certainly also linked to the combination of intellectual curiosity and a limited attention span. Someone, maybe a Belgian, said that the French can solve any problem, assuming that they can detect the problem in the first place. I mentioned this to a Dutch multinational executive and he added: "If I give the French a problem to solve, they come back with a different problem..."

Of course the ability to revise one's thinking over time should not be interpreted by foreigners as an act of rank perfidy but rather as a natural consequence of French cartesianism allied with a reluctance to commit things to paper. E Russell Eggers, an American businessman with a great sensitivity toward the cultures of Europe, commented that "the Frenchman, by inclination and education, mistrusts simple things and tends to over-complicate. It is for this reason that no Frenchman, by American standards, can ask a simple, straightforward question when speaking in public." To which he added: "Whereas the American tries to think in a straight line, the Frenchman insists on thinking in a circle." By comparison the Belgian, like an Italian, will think tangentially but still get there.

In fact it's funny how often the 'circle' analogy comes up when foreigners discuss the French. In her book *French or Foe* Polly Platt quotes an American computer engineer who commented to her that the French "swim in circles": their bodies are evidently taking instructions from their brains. Polly then went on to discuss the prevalence of circles in French public life: starting from the *rond point* of L'Etoile, Paris itself is a set of concentric circles, to which I would add that, viewed from outer space, the 'Hexagon' looks almost circular too.

This is appropriate for a traditionally centralised country where, in the words of American interculturalist Edward Hall, even "the man in charge of a French office can often be found in the middle, with his minions placed like satellites on strings radiating outward from him." Commenting on the French fondness for protest Anne-Elisabeth Moutet, a French journalist, says that "revolution in France always obeys the strict laws of physics: it is a complete rotation until one stands exactly where one did before."

Despite their claims to cartesianism, the French are often circumlocutory in both their thinking and speech. However they are also delightfully self-aware, as the comment by Anne-Elisabeth Moutet indicates. Take this comment by Jack Lang, French Minister of Culture in the Mitterand administration: "The French always go from the general to the particular. The Anglo-Saxons start with a concrete fact and reason from that. They call a cat a cat. We like to blah-blah-blah."

It looks as if today's French should be regretting their attachment to their supposed Celtic origins: *"nos ancêtres les Gaulois"* as the history books once claimed. The Celts were a pretty quarrelsome lot, also spending much of their time going around in circles and using convoluted mental constructions for simple things: sixty-ten *(soixante-dix)* for 70 and four-twenties *(quatre-vingt)* for 80. French-speaking Belgians just say *'septante'* for 70, but stop at the *'ottante'* favoured by the French Swiss.

Unfortunately a lot of Gallic protest these days seems to be a static and sterile resistance to change. One of the worst things French society ever did was come up with the concept of the *acquis*, established rights or, to the cynical British mind, vested interests – an idea that has been put to better use by the European Union.

It's a great thing to focus on *acquis* when you're trying to build something but, once you've built it, it degenerates into a selfish, unproductive 'dog-in-the-manger' syndrome. The French, after all, had their real revolutions centuries ago, although we are still feeling the aftershocks. But when French unions go on strike in response to a government proposal to abolish a one-day public holiday and use the revenue for a national solidarity fund to provide healthcare for the elderly, the *acquis* attitude looks obscene. It's not one that is shared by Belgian union folk, who are less doctrinaire and more humane.

One of the things that unites French, British and Americans, however, is the belief that 'information is power'.

In business, people will often withhold information until they are forced to divulge it. A senior manager with the old Compaq organisation told me that, on conference phone calls between the US headquarters and its French and German subsidiaries, the American and French ends frequently had unannounced participants keeping quiet at the back of the room and taking notes. The Germans eventually complained of unfair play!

10. Neighbours – the Germans

"The Germans always buy platform tickets before they storm a railway station"

German satirist Kurt Tucholsky (falsely attributed to Lenin)

Compared with the Belgians, the Germans are too organised.

Driving up through the *Ostkantone* on the motorway to Aachen prepares you for what lies ahead. There is an orderliness about the architecture that contrasts starkly with the anarchy you are leaving behind you.

In my earlier book *We Europeans* I dwelt on two aspects of the German psyche: the importance of what I call the 'Social Consensus Effect' (SCE) and the significance of a sense of mysticism as a balance to the compelling need for order and discipline in the German mind. Ultimately, it all comes back to organisation.

It was only a few years ago that I became aware of an equally dominant factor, a sense of territoriality. This was brought to my notice in two ways. First, I happened to read what Edward Hall, the American anthropologist, had to say about this in his book *Understanding Cultural Differences*: "Many Germans feel hemmed in geographically. For the German, space is sacred. Homes are protected from outsiders by a variety of barriers: fences, walls, hedges, solid doors, blinds, shutters and screening to prevent visual or auditory intrusion." Sounds a bit like the Belgians...

Secondly, I was exposed to the phenomenon personally when I unwittingly took a table in a self-service restaurant that a German had already appropriated for himself. I had wrongly assumed that the copy of *Bild Zeitung* he had left there on his way back to the service counter had simply been abandoned. But no, this was the way he staked his claim. Maybe it would have been different if I had asked him if I could share his table: after all, Germans are often politer than foreigners.

At about the same time (and very belatedly by many people's standards) I became aware of the stories told by the British about the Germans and bathing towels. You know the scenario: on holiday the Brits stagger down to the swimming pool with awful hangovers and find all the Germans already there with their towels laid out in the sunniest spots. This story has now achieved the status of an urban myth, yet it is too close to reality never to have happened. Moreover it has been the subject of a hilarious commercial by Carling Beer, shown only on British television of course...

In the year 2000 the INRA research company conducted an opinion poll across the country. One of the questions posed to respondents was (I lie not): "Do you want a fence round your garden?" A foreigner might think this is a trivial issue for a public opinion survey, but evidently not.

No less than 82 per cent of East Germans said 'yes' to the proposition, while 56 per cent of West German respondents also concurred.

Asked in a separate poll by the Allensbach Institute whether they considered freedom more important than equality, 51 percent of West Germans agreed with the proposition against only 29 per cent of East Germans. If 'Ossis' think equality is that important, you might think they would also be prepared to share their gardens with their neighbours...

The most eloquent confirmation of this German sense of territoriality and garden limits came in a German TV interview I witnessed just after the dramatic floods of 2002. One of the unfortunate victims, a resident of Saxony, told his interviewer that, in order to reach his property, he had asked his neighbour for permission to *row over his back garden*!

Innocent foreigners might have thought that the pressure of events – or the fact that it must have been difficult to determine the neighbour's territorial limits when they lay under a couple of meters of water – would have rendered the request irrelevant, but no! Instinct allied with a natural German sense of politeness prevailed.

Less polite was a suspect in a German *Krimi* TV film who addressed intruding police inspectors with the words: *"Verlassen Sie mein Grundstück!"* ("leave my piece of ground!"). Territoriality again.

Probably, though, the context for the most excruciating sense of territoriality is the German car, which is not just the individual's symbol of 'freedom' but an extremely tangible extension of his or her human rights. Touch a German car with your little finger and the driver is likely to get out to check the damage to the paintwork. Bump a German car when you're trying to park and – unlike the average French driver who will just shrug his shoulders – you'll probably find yourself in a fight or in court, or both.

Ultimately, territoriality is linked to the German urge to compartmentalise things. Give a German politician a new issue, and he or she will create a committee *(Ausschuss)*. Even unmanageable things like the day's news get the same treatment: they are broken up into bits, or *'Themen'*, in a way that deprives them of their topicality but makes them assimilable for the well regimented German mind. They are often 'packaged' in the process. In my naughtier moments, I like to think that packet-switching, a means of distributing information faster, was a German invention. It was not. It was American but, then, they have well organised minds too.

'Ossis' versus 'Wessis'

The INRA and Allensbach polls show the enormous gulf that separates the East and West Germans. The 2002 federal elections helped drive the reality home: there are big differences in the way of thinking and the underlying value systems of the Ossis and Wessis.

This reality has always intrigued me. It poses the kind of dilemma that bears comparison with that other great cultural 'what-dun-it?': what was it that turned the footloose Vikings into land-hungry Normans?

The incompatibility of the two sides of Germany was evident even before the Wall came down. At the time it simply looked like a typical standoff between the 'haves' and the 'have nots'. Now it doesn't look so simple. There is a fundamental lack of empathy, sometimes mistrust and even outright animosity between the two. The Ossis think the Wessis are spoiled and arrogant, the Wessis think the Ossis are ungracious and unappreciative (they are certainly less generous and rather intolerant).

How did all this come about? I have difficulty in accepting the idea that it is all the work of the social environment created by such a rotten and, in historical terms, short-lived regime as the German Democratic Republic - a regime that regularly prompted my ex-East-German brother-in-law to mutter, parrot-like, *"alle Verbrecher"* ("all criminals"). Admittedly Ulbricht, Honecker and henchmen did have some good things going like subsidised meals and free crèches (something that Wessis sadly lack) to offer the rank and file. But it seems to me that such strong cultural divergences have to be found further back in history.

I still have this theory that Old Fritz' and Bismarck's Prussia had something to do with it, although my German critics make the point that Prussia's boundaries quickly extended well beyond the frontiers of East Germany.

Yet my suspicions are reinforced by the following paragraph in Gordon Craig's book *The Germans*: "In the state of Brandenburg-Prussia an important difference is to be noted. Here, while the bulk of the population remained Lutheran, the ruling Hohenzollern dynasty was converted in 1613 to Calvinism [which] brought into the country... ideas of *raison d'état*, of science of government, and of State growth..." In the same section Craig talks about "active obedience and service to the state" which certainly sounds like the Prussia I have read about - but not at all like the Ossis of today!

So the mystery remains, for me, a mystery. In the meantime, the Berlin Wall has been replaced by a wall in men's (and women's) heads...

Dogs versus children

If the Belgians know how to treat their children but not how to train their dogs (Chapter 2), the opposite seems to apply to the Germans. I commented in *WeEuropeans* on the traditionally stern attitude of Germans towards their kids – which has been categorised by some German observers as *Kinderfeindlichkeit* ('animosity towards children'). I used to feel this was somewhat overstating the case, but have since concluded that the truth lies, as usual, halfway between the two.

In his book *Germany and the Germans*, the British author John Ardagh ventured the idea that it might have something to do with "failure to understand a child's imaginative world." As an ardent fan of children's programmes on German television, I also find this argument unacceptable: I think Germans always had this ability but, in the past, they used it more to moralise (viz *Struwelpeter*) than to entertain.

It is certainly true that German children of the current generation can be so boisterous and uninhibited that they disturb the natural German order. It is also true that German dogs, compared with Belgian dogs, are extremely well behaved. Not only are they less inclined to litter the sidewalks with their visiting cards (except in Berlin), they are also taught not to interrupt: since 1992 the dogs in the small city of Hamm (human population: 190,000) have been prohibited from barking between 7 pm and 8 am. In many restaurants, dogs are welcome but children not...

It is certainly true that many older Germans seem to be more indulgent to dogs than to children. A Scots friend of mine has lived for a number of years in both Germany and Italy. When I asked him to give his impressions of the differences of life in the two countries, he said laconically: "To get to know people in Germany, buy yourself a dog. To get to know people in Italy, get a pram with a baby in it."

In a feature in the *International Herald Tribune* in the year 2000 Stacy Wiedenmann, an American expatriate married to a German, confirmed my Scots friend's experience: "Perhaps Germans like dogs more than kids – certainly they talk to you through dogs. I think they feel more comfortable because a child is personal, perhaps too personal. So a dog becomes the ideal passport to social contact."

This feature led to an animated exchange of correspondence in 'letters to the editor' which culminated in a comment from another American expatriate: "I have lived in Germany for 20 years and have witnessed countless incidents displaying pro-dog and anti-children behavior. One particular incident sticks out: an irate shopper at a grocery store screamed at a mother to make her crying infant (who was probably merely hungry) be quiet. The shopper added: 'I have a small dog at home, and he doesn't make any noise.' When I asked her if she had never cried when she was a child, she replied, almost proudly: 'No! And it was forbidden for us to be loud.'"

The moral must simply be this: dogs are easier to control than children, unless you're Belgian..

... and that little matter of humour

A popular Dutch joke concerns the Belgian visitor to Amsterdam who goes up to a local and asks: "Excuse me, but is this the third street to the left."

While the English seem to concede that the Dutch, and even the Belgians, may share something of their own sense of humour, generations of my compatriots – and quite a lot of other western Europeans - live happily with the idea that the Germans are bereft of any such thing. They rarely have occasion to check out for themselves. Most of them don't speak German, other than words like *'Achtung'* and *'Ordnung'*, and some of them have never even met a

German in the flesh (not always an edifying sight if you've been on holiday to the Costa Blanca). But the Brits still stick fervently to this idea, partly out of a sense of superiority: having a sense of humour is a great source of English competitive pride, the Germans having shown they're better at most other things like building automobiles and running railways.

A very perceptive official from the US Treasury once pointed out to me that most cultural quirks need to be placed in context, in other words that *context is as important as culture*. As examples of this, the English are conciliatory as individuals, but extremely disputatious in public scenarios like the House of Commons, international diplomacy and the courts of law; the Dutch are careful with their money in their day-to-day lives (though less and less so), but very generous in meaningful situations like end-of-year gifts for family and friends, or Third World aid; and the Germans resort to humour in normal social circumstances but tend to eschew it when involved in negotiations or discussing business. I suspect the UK's business community is as much to blame as anyone else for keeping this old chestnut in the fire…

Gone are the days when, as a German friend of mine put it, "for us Germans, humour is no laughing matter." The fact is that German humour, when displayed, is every bit as lively as English humour, without achieving the sheer range of the latter. I learned this when writing *Sharks & Custard* about the different styles of humour in Europe: the chapter on German humour turned out to be the longest in the book. In the meantime I have had my convictions confirmed by the results of the British *LaughLab* experiment which found that, out of ten nationalities, it was the Germans who found the jokes funnier than any of the other respondents and, moreover, came out in the study as the happiest.

The *LaughLab* experiment rated the following as the two best German jokes:

A general noticed one of his soldiers behaving oddly. The soldier would pick up any piece of paper he found, frown and say: 'That's not it' and put it down again. This went on for some time, until the general arranged to have the soldier psychologically tested. The psychologist concluded that the soldier was deranged, and wrote out his discharge from the army. The soldier picked it up, smiled and said: 'That's it'.

Scientists have shown that the moon is moving away at a tiny, although measurable, distance from the Earth every year. If you do the maths, you can calculate that 85 million years ago the moon was orbiting the Earth at a distance of about 35 feet from the Earth's surface. This would explain the death of the dinosaurs – the tallest ones, anyway.

Who says Germans don't have a sense of humour? There's even a German sanitary ware company that stencils houseflies on its urinals. Well, at least that shows a sense of fun...

P.S. While I'm about it...

Why does German TV specialise in:

1. soaps with doctors and other professionals in white coats?
2. constant references to the *Grundgesetz* (constitution) and the *Verfassungsgericht* (constitutional court)?
3. talk shows where elderly German gentlemen go on boringly about party politics (and of course the constitution and the constitutional court)?
4. celebrity shows with the same old faces?
5. music spectaculars where the audience always starts clapping rhythmically as soon as the band strikes up (unless it's Beethoven)?

The curious thing is that the talk show hosts and the entertainers are often Austrian or Dutch...

Hmm!

Brussels, Belgium and **Beyond**

11. Neighbours – the English

"The problem with the Belgians is that they can't tell the difference between tax avoidance and tax evasion."

British expatriate lawyer

Compared with the Belgians, the English are too insular.

In addition to the fact that we English often have difficulty in acknowledging we are part of the European sub-continent, itself an appendage of Asia (after all, only some 8,000 years ago, there was still a land bridge linking the islands to the mainland), we are often hasty, even faulty, in our judgement of foreigners.

Foreigners, too, have problems in understanding us.
For a start there is confusion over definitions: 'English' is essentially a cultural term (I hesitate to add 'ethnic', since we're a very mongrel lot), 'British' a political one, primarily thanks to the Act of Union with Scotland in 1707. There are big differences between the culture I am talking about here and the Celtic ones represented by the people of Wales, Scotland, Ireland and, up to a point (Landsend), Cornwall. Apart from anything else, the Celts are more likely to say what they mean...

Ask many Continentals the most appropriate word to describe us and they will say, without hesitation: 'hypocritical'! I know, because I have put the question many times and this is the answer I generally get.

We English have done as good a job in trying to give ourselves a positive but tendentious image as we have done in giving the Belgians and the Dutch negative ones. After all, it was we who invented the word 'fair', a word that has found its way into the French and German languages to make up for the lack of a local equivalent. It obviously suits us to think that we are a fair-minded people and, in many ways, it fits with our reputation for tolerance and reasonably reasoned argument. But is it true?

For a start we were not very fair in the 17th century when we said terrible things about the Dutch (see Chapter 8). In the words of the late lamented humorist George Mikes: "If you want to be really and truly British, you must become a hypocrite" (he really meant 'English'). Margaret Atwood, the Canadian novelist, hinted at the same thing: "I know the British are famed for their plots, not saying what they really mean..." (she meant 'English' too).

American sociologists Philip Harris and Robert Moran concur in their book *Managing Cultural Differences* when they say: "For all their simulated modesty, the British can be tough and blandly ruthless when necessary. They are masters at intelligence, political blackmail and chicanery." (they meant 'English' as well). Robert-Jan Van Ogtrop, a South African businessman, says much the same thing, but is maybe a bit more complimentary: "It's very difficult to understand what the English are really saying, what they really mean. They're great artists, great actors." (Hats off to him, he says 'English'...).

Italian journalist and author Luigi Barzini refers in his book *The Europeans* to the ability of British statesmen (NB we're talking politics here) to "resort with equal ease and elegance to what seemed to foreigners Levantine duplicity, Greek ambiguities, Florentine intrigues and, but more rarely, outright treachery. This unexpected flexibility", he added, "offended the French in particular, perhaps because they alone felt entitled to resort to such dubious techniques."

The impression we English give has also been acknowledged by no less eminent an Englishman than the late Lord Hailsham who said: "The British are notable for their sentimentality, which they mistake for a virtue: hence their ability to deceive themselves, which others mistake for hypocrisy." This sounds subtle enough (even if he confused 'British' with 'English'), but I feel the real explanation may be subtler still.

The underlying reality is that, as individuals, we English are conciliatory by nature. Those of us who have received anything resembling a real education (and of course there are lots of exceptions) have been brought up *not to make a fuss*. That in itself is curious since in public scenarios, such as the law courts or the House of Commons, we go out of our way to be quite the opposite, i.e. highly competitive and adversarial.

Yet it is in our real nature to keep a stiff upper lip and swallow hard, even under duress. To use another analogy, we paint ourselves into an emotional corner... and are then forced to fight our way out. This comes as a great surprise to foreigners who have been expecting us to say what we really think, and consequently tax us with hypocrisy. Yet all we have been trying to do is keep the peace. In this respect we are not unlike the Finns who, contrary to popular belief, are very emotional people but generally keep their feelings to themselves more successfully than the English.

On reflection, I'm inclined to think we English invented the concept of fairness precisely because it stands out in contrast to the high degree of skulduggery practised by some of our own people. We certainly have a great facility for being mealy-mouthed. Some of the grosser examples of English pseudo-speak include the following (taken from a Dutch guide to English posted on a wall at the European Court of Justice!):

Correct me if I'm wrong	=	Please don't contradict me!
I'll bear it in mind	=	I'll do nothing about it.
By the way	=	The primary purpose of our discussion is...
Up to a point	=	No, definitely not!
With the greatest respect	=	I think you're stupid.
I'm thinking about it	=	Forget it!

and of course there is also the infamous:

We must have lunch some time	=	I hope I never see you again.

"You hear many Americans during their first year in London tell their British counterparts: why can't you talk straight?" says a US banker interviewed by the *Financial Times*. "The British indirect manner of speech winds up American colleagues enormously." Not just Americans either (who, it seems, also can't tell the difference between the British and the English...).

The younger generations have progressively turned their backs on traditional English understatement. Their powers of expression, such as they are, seem to focus on superlatives like 'brilliant', 'fantastic' and, increasingly, 'awesome'. They have gone to the other end of the emotional scale, but the result's just the same. We're still not saying what we really mean...

At the end of the day...

Watching German TV commentaries, I have always been surprised at the number of times the interviewee takes refuge behind the words *"Im Grunde genommen..."* (i.e. 'basically' or 'fundamentally'). The Germans are, after all, a very fundamental people.

But is only recently that I have become aware of a comparable verbal loophole favoured by the English: "At the end of the day...". This is what one would reasonably expect of Europe's ultimate empiricists – namely that, when all the verbalising is over and done with, that's the way things are... and nobody can do anything about it.

Of course, it's not just the English who use their language to communicate and mis-communicate. French-speaking Belgians have a wonderful glossary of multifunctional adverbs. These include:

Instamment	=	get on with it (even if we don't).
Normalement	=	if all things were equal (which they aren't), you could expect it by..... (but you can't).
Fatalement	=	it's a real mess, I can't do anything about it.
Incessamment	=	in the next month or so.
Momentanément	=	for a long time.

Such weasel words, or catch-phrases, can be found in most European languages. They reveal the underlying predispositions of people and can be helpful in deciphering differing trains of thought.

In the case of 'at the end of the day', this English catchphrase conceals a deep-set aversion to any theoretical or predetermined solutions. Ultimately it reflects an underlying resistance to the formalised regulation of life, a resistance that dates back to the time of the Romans. This led to a refusal by the English to accept the principles of Roman law, namely the codification of everything that society found unacceptable, and to the subsequent development of the Common Law system in preference to the Roman or Napoleonic Code.

According to the fifth-century Byzantine historian Zosimus, the Britons, preoccupied with fighting off barbarian invaders, divested themselves very rapidly of the influences of Roman civilisation. What is certain is that later on, with the arrival of the Normans, as recorded by Robert Lopez in *The Birth of Europe*, "by order of King Stephen (1135-1154)... books of canon and civil law were confiscated and the teaching of the subject forbidden. If the English jurists wished to create a doctrine valid for the kingdom, they were to base it not on imported generalizations but on local precedents, feudal customs, court decisions and royal statutes."

No wonder then that, seven centuries later, Thomas Carlyle was able to say in his book *The French Revolution*: "Of the continental nuisance called 'Bureaucracy' I can see no risk or possibility in England." No wonder the Brits don't like Brussels!

In making the statement cited at the head of this chapter, a British lawyer friend was implying that tax avoidance was perfectly proper but tax evasion was reprehensible: in fact, the Belgians can tell the difference between the two. My friend may also have been paying a tacit compliment to the Belgian tax administration which adopts a pragmatic and sensible approach, rare in the offshore islands these days, to the business of 'claiming the state's share'. Official evidence of this is provided by the existence of a federal government unit that offers a confidential one-stop service to minimise the fiscal consequences for any business setting up in the country! In fact, from my personal experience, the biggest tax evaders here have been my fellow-Brits...

The kneejerk reaction typical of many Little Englanders to such continental casuistry was evident in the outburst of a Tory MP, Patrick Nicholls, who said back in the mid-90s (with scant regard for the European Union's institutional geography): "This really is the last straw. It's yet another example of countries, many of whom have a deplorable record on human rights, presuming to lecture our Home Secretary and our courts. The British people are fed up with our courts being overruled by a bunch of academic civil servants in Strasbourg who do not understand our legal system." Harrumph!

Nothing venture...

Some years ago I was asked to advise a British company on their differences with a Belgian partner in a joint-venture construction project. They were concerned about their partner's response to two issues. The first had been an opportunity to upgrade the specifications agreed with the client: the British had come up with a number of options that would give a comparable, or superior, solution at less cost, but the Belgians refused to consider any of these options and stuck rigidly to the specifications. The second related to safety precautions. The British examined the risks

> *involved and came up with measures exceeding the legal*
> *minima, whereas the Belgians stuck strictly to the*
> *legislation, observing the letter of the law where the*
> *British honoured the spirit. This struck me as untypical,*
> *knowing the Belgian capacity for compromise, until I*
> *realised that the problem here was one of corporate*
> *cultures – the Belgian partner was part of a big*
> *bureaucratic group – and not one of 'national' cultures.*

The ultimate eccentrics

Common law has helped give the British what Professor
Geert Hofstede calls 'low uncertainty avoidance' which can
also be roughly described as a high tolerance of ambiguity.
In 1995 Dr David Weeks, a Welsh-American clinical
neuropsychologist, and American journalist Jamie James
wrote a book called *Eccentrics*. This recorded the findings
of a study undertaken over the previous decade into the
qualities that characterise eccentricity.

How they determined who was eccentric and who was not
proved to be a very pragmatic process. As they say in their
introduction: "Exactly how much deviation from the norm
it takes to qualify as a true eccentric is a vexed issue: until
we have established qualitatively what eccentricity is, then
it is impossible to contemplate the issue quantitatively. For
eccentricity is a trait that everyone partakes of to a greater
or lesser extent: absolute, uniform conformity, if it existed,
would itself be a kind of eccentricity." The latter, if it exists

anywhere, is to be found in Germany as what I choose to call the Social Consensus Effect (see Chapter 10). Perhaps, as the pioneers of precision engineering, it is hardly surprising that the Germans show the least deviation from the norm.

Dr Weeks is emphatic about his study's conclusions: "Britain and Holland have by far the greatest number of eccentrics in Europe. I estimate there is one eccentric for every 10,000 people in Britain. The figure for Europe as a whole is only half that, and Germany has the fewest eccentrics of all." For reasons given earlier in this book most Belgians, university professors excepted, avoid demonstrations of eccentricity.

The study's findings endorse these countries' ratings on Hofstede's Uncertainty Avoidance index, where Britain again comes out at one end of the scale (the highest tolerance of ambiguity of the three) and Germany at the other (the lowest). It seems reasonable that tolerance of ambiguity would encourage eccentricity.

The Belgians don't like uncertainty any more than the others, but they have learned to live with it. They are also expert at creating ambiguity by keeping their opinions to themselves...

Oh, sense of humour? Sure. My favourite Belgian joke is one which, almost inevitably, takes a pot shot at the country's neighbours to the south:

A Frenchman goes into a bar with a parrot on his shoulder, and the parrot is wearing a baseball cap. 'Hey,' says the

barman,' that's neat! Where did you get him?' 'France,' says
the parrot, 'they've got millions of them there.'

It's a joke that has to be Belgian. It's funny, not cruel,
amiable, just like them.

The last word...

*I maybe belong to that generation of Flemings that
no longer really relates to the linguistic struggle.
I get angry when I think back to the time we were
always being told we had to defend ourselves against
the others. Just as if they wanted us to believe in
Father Christmas.*

(Ik behoor wellicht tot die generatie Vlamingen die
niet echt meer een boodschap heeft aan de taalstrijd.
Ik ben boos als ik terugdenk aan de tijd dat men ons
altijd heeft voorgehouden dat we ons moesten verdedigen
tegen de andere. Net alsof men ons wijsmaakte dat
Sinterklaas bestond.)

Wim Delvoye, Flemish conceptual artist.

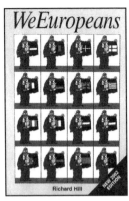

WeEuropeans – the international bestseller

(5th revised and updated 2005 edition)
432 pages
Format 195 x 130 mm (7 3/4 x 5")
ISBN 90-74440-11-8

This book has been extensively revised and updated since the launch of the first edition in 1992. 'WeEuropeans' rapidly became a non-fiction bestseller and over 60,000 copies have now been sold worldwide.

Chapters describe in an anecdotal and easy-to-read style, supported by research results and input from a wide range of observers, the finer points that distinguish one European culture from another. The book provides a penetrating and entertaining analysis of the attitudes and behavioural traits of each nationality.

"Wonderful stuff. Witty and accurate without being cynical"
John Mole, author of "Mind Your Manners"

"I've thoroughly enjoyed your book. It's a rare gift to combine scholarly insights with a witty compelling style!"
John Humble, management consultant

"Richard Hill starts from the obvious to discover the difficult and makes an impressive success of it."
Emanuele Gazzo, Agence Europe

"This book is for those who are interested in going a little deeper into those peculiar national traits that often burst to the surface in a character. You will find many examples of national habits and tendencies which you may vaguely have noticed before but could not really put your finger on. Not only are these traits described (which in itself is hilarious to read), but they are also, where possible, convincingly explained. Hill leaves you the impression that he has seen a great deal, but what does he make of it all? I think the idea is to extract as much amusement as possible from the variety of habits throughout Europe and to avoid taking these differences too seriously. If there's one chap needed in a sensible future European Parliament, then it is him. This book is simply fantastic!"
From: amazon.co.uk

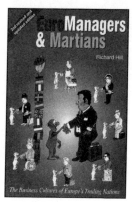

EuroManagers & Martians

(3rd revised and updated 2002 edition)
272 pages
Format 195 x 130 mm (7 3/4 x 5")
ISBN 90-74440-13-4

Richard Hill has brought to this book a lifetime's experience as a consultant to business and industry, reinforced by the opinions and conclusions of more than 1,000 senior international executives.

Hill looks closely at the business and management cultures of Europe. He identifies those areas where cultures collide, comparing management styles and negotiating strategies, and analysing the implications of cross-frontier strategic alliances, multicultural teamwork and 'New Age' management techniques.

In the final chapter he examines the case for the EuroManager – as yet an unverified life form like 'little green men' – and concludes that, for the present at any rate, the sensible solution is still to 'Think Global, Act Local'.

"The book is written from an alien"s point of view, and it presents both carefully researched and anecdotal evidence in an entertaining read... Carefully steering a course away from the stereotype path, Hill gives well-considered and practical advice on conducting Eurobusiness."

The European

"A shrewd commentary on the real Europe, the Europe of enterprising men and women. Anyone looking for an intelligent, digestible and readable book should buy it."

Trends

"As an Australian in Europe trying to study and work, this book (EuroManagers & Martians) provided me with some fantastic tips on what and what not to do when!! The mix of anecdotes and factual content means that it is very readable and the relaxed style and humour are very refreshing! A thoroughly enjoyable and informative read"!

From: amazon.com

Great Britain Little England

152 pages
Format 195 x 130 mm (7 3/4 x 5")
ISBN 90-74440-04-5

In his fourth book in this series, Richard Hill takes a look at his own country. In 152 pages he puts the foibles of the English under the microscope, examining the suspicion of things like vision and long-term planning, and the attachment to class, chumminess and ceremonial
.

Hill insists that the English have enormous reserves of creativity and industry, but fail to maximise them: "There is so much talent and promise locked up in this little island that failure to exploit it ranks as little less than a crime against humanity - both against the birthright of the English and against the right of foreigners to enjoy what the English could bring to life if only their system gave them the chance".

"It should be required reading, considering the isolationist attitudes which still too often persist among senior executives"

EuroBusiness

The NewComers
The Austrians, Finns and Swedes

176 pages
Format 195 x 130 mm (7 3/4 x 5")
ISBN 90-74440-06-1

Austria, Finland and Sweden are now well established and influential members of the European Union, yet ignorance about these countries is as great as ever. Richard Hill joined forces with journalist David Haworth to write The NewComers, a book that 'takes the lid off' the citizens of these three countries - their virtues, their quirks, tastes, habits and sensitivities, and relevant background on history and politics.

"I would like to congratulate you on this publication, which is not only a delightful read, but gives at the same time a very comprehensive insight into these countries, their people and mentalities"
Austrian Embassy Official

"Delightful! You seem to have got the essence of this extremely complex society"

British businesswoman in Vienna

Us & Them
172 pages - Format 195 x 130 mm (7 3/4 x 5")
74440-10-X

In his book *"Us & Them"* Richard Hill examines European separatism in its various forms: the regionalist movement, attitudes to minorities, the bonding instinct and, most significantly, the silent separatism that has distanced the younger generations of Europeans from the world of politics.

Since his first book *"WeEuropeans"* came onto the market, Hill has had the opportunity to address audiences of students, undergraduates and graduates totalling over 15,000 young people of every European nationality.

In discussing European issues with them, he discovered that these young people have largely disengaged from conventional politics. They regard politicians with, at best, disinterest and, at worst, distaste or disrespect. This attitude is prevalent across all western European countries, with the possible exception of the Netherlands and Ireland.

Hill concludes: "The world has changed massively in the last fifty years, but western Europe still lives with the threat of social dislocation. Then, the problem was the divides that separated countries and cultures. Us was the mother-country, Them was the rest. Now, the dislocation is within countries and cultures, the growing gulf between Europe's young people and the society they were born into. Today Us is Europe's youth and Them is the rest of us".

Hill's conclusions are supported by the findings of national and international opinion studies, reviewed in detail in the book.

"I found this new book to be as exciting and witty as ever. I'll steal stuff from it if you don't mind, but will always give you credit!"
Gilles de Courtivron, Professor, McGregor School of Business, Ohio

"This is an astonishing book, not only because of the superbly lucid and vigorous writing, but also because the thoughts are equally rigorous and right in both form and substance. I have recommended it to my students."
Adelino Torres, Professor, Universidade Tecnica de Lisboa

They Only Laughed Later
Tales of Women On the Move

Co-edited by Carol Allen and Richard Hill.
214 pages
Format 195 x 130 mm (7 3/4 x 5")
ISBN 90-74440-12-6

This collection of essays is the product of a series of 'Women On the Move' conferences, which brought together expatriate women from over twenty countries. Their concerns were mutual: to share experience in meeting the challenges that confront women who move to strange lands in pursuit of their own or their husbands' careers.

Some of this experience is resumed in this collection of essays, many of them written by published authors, all of whom were fresh from one or more assignments abroad. While there may seem precious little to laugh about in the midst of so much mobility, the truth is that hilarity lurks in the corners of most moves. Aspects of expatriate life evoked in the book include general culture shock, homesickness, language confusion, change of climate, adaptation to cultural differences, and repatriation.

"They Only Laughed Later" is a pat-on-the-back and a keep-up-the-good-spirits to all the women who have made and are making the most of living abroad. It is a gentle prod, an outstretched hand, a go-for-it to those who find coping abroad scary and insurmountable.

Each of the 30 essays is a heartfelt cameo taken from the real-life experience of an expatriate.

Sharks and Custard

Sharks and Custard
The Things That Make Europeans Laugh
190 pages - Format 195 x 130 mm (7 3/4 x 5")
ISBN 90-74440-14-2

In his last book Sharks and Custard Richard Hill set out to do two things: first, throw light on the different styles of humor of the English, the French, the Germans etc, and, secondly, offer a careful selection of what he thinks are the best jokes by and about the countries concerned.

For Hill, Sharks and Custard is a logical progression from the spadework he did on European cultures in his earlier bestsellers, *WeEuropeans* and *EuroManagers and Martians*. Humor is an important component of international business life that needs to be handled with tact and understanding. At best it can defuse the difficult moments of a major negotiation, at worst it can ruin a relationship!

If the title of the book needs explanation, that is deliberate. Behind it lies a classic English joke – "Question: What is yellow and dangerous? Answer: Shark-infested custard." – a joke that makes foreigners feel culturally challenged. Custard is a traditional English sweet which should rightfully be as famous as pudding, but isn't...

".... a perceptive analysis of German humor and, especially, of one of its essential components, self-deprecating Jewish humor -a fundamental element in the humor of all central European countries."
Polly Platt, author of the best-selling French or Foe? and Savoir-Flair!

"El libro no nos dejó dormir anoche. Estuvimos leyendo en la cama algunos capítulos y nos gustaron sobre todo los chistes irlandeses."
Mariano Garcia Landa, International Interpreter, Spain

"The book is hilarious!"
Alan Tillier, Journalist, France

"Ich hätte nie gedacht, daß man über so etwas Heiteres wie Witze und Bonmots so viel Ernstes und Nachdenkliches sagen kann, daß man daran sogar eine tiefschürfende Analyse in vergleichender Völkerpsychologie knüpfen kann."
Klaus Müller, Author of Den Urlaub überleben, Germany

"This is a great book because it is not just a list of jokes but jokes in a social and cultural context."
Andrzej Szoszkiewicz, Editor, BM Magazine, Poland